ALL B

Samantha Lee is a woman of many parts. She not only acts, sings, lectures and broadcasts, but she also writes novels. She has long been an active enthusiast in the field of health and fitness, and is the author of *Fit to be Fifty*. She lives in London with her teenage son and an extremely vocal finch.

Also by Samantha Lee

FIT TO BE FIFTY

ALL BY MYSELF

HOW TO PICK UP THE PIECES WHEN YOUR MAN HAS GONE

SAMANTHA LEE

VISTA

First published in Great Britain 1996
as a Vista paperback original

Vista is an imprint of the Cassell Group
Wellington House, 125 Strand, London WC2R 0BB

© Samantha Lee 1996

The right of Samantha Lee to be identified as author of
this work has been asserted by her in accordance with
the Copyright, Designs and Patents Act, 1988.

A catalogue record for this book is
available from the British Library.

ISBN 0 575 60083 7

Typeset by Textype, Cambridge
Printed and bound in Great Britain
by Cox & Wyman Ltd, Reading, Berks

All rights reserved. No part of this publication may be
reproduced or transmitted in any form or by any means,
electronic or mechanical including photocopying,
recording or any information storage or retrieval system,
without prior permission in writing from the publishers.

This book is sold subject to the condition that it shall not,
by way of trade or otherwise, be lent, resold, hired out, or
otherwise circulated without the publisher's prior consent
in any form of binding or cover other than that in which it
is published and without a similar condition including this
condition being imposed on the subsequent purchaser.

96 97 98 99   10 9 8 7 6 5 4 3 2 1

*To Ben and Emily
with love*

Contents

Acknowledgements	page 9
How to Use this Book	11
Prologue	13
1 Making a Drama out of a Crisis: Why Not?	19
2 An Attitude of Gratitude	26
Survival Strategy 1: How to Relax	34
3 Accentuate the Positive	38
4 Priorities	46
Survival Strategy 2: Creative Visualization	54
5 All the Things You Are	61
6 I Thought as Much!	66
Survival Strategy 3: Keep in Touch	72
7 Beat the Abandonment Blues	75
8 Massaging the Ego	82
Survival Strategy 4: Fit For Life	88
9 Home Sweet Home	91
10 Financial Fitness: Part I	103
Survival Strategy 5: Cut-Price Cookery	111
11 Financial Fitness: Part II	119
12 Financial Fitness: Part III	125
Survival Strategy 6: Affirmations	132

13	Do You Sincerely Want Another Man?	139
14	Connections	151
	Survival Strategy 7: Yoga	157
15	Moving On	160
16	Moving In	168
	Survival Strategy 8: Sanctuary	171
17	DIY for Idiots	182
18	Goal-Setting	191
	Survival Strategy 9: Eating for Energy	197
19	Self-Support	204
20	Business Sense	213
	Survival Strategy 10: Futures Checklist	223
	Epilogue	227
	Further Reading	229
	Useful Addresses	231

Acknowledgements

My overwhelming thanks to my good friends who listened, and listened, and listened: Doris and Moira and Maggie and Jack and Charlie and Garry. To my accountant Frank Dunphy and Cameron Ameira, then manager of the Union Street Branch of the Bradford and Bingley Building Society, for making sure I had a roof over my head. To the wonderful Eileen for keeping the house from falling apart while I was. And last but not least to my supportive, funny, handsome, wok-wielding, computer-gaming, light-bulb-changing, science-fiction-fan son, Stevie, who gave me something to fight for and who never took sides.

How to Use This Book

All by Myself is about coping after you've been left in the lurch by someone you love. It's a book about recovery and growth, about beating the bad times and emerging wiser and stronger. It's about the future. *Your* future.

Throughout the text you'll find 'Survival Strategies' designed to help you through the long dark night of abandonment. You can swallow these in one gulp or dip into them at your leisure. Try them all or just the ones that appeal to you. Nothing is obligatory.

This is not a book about musts or shoulds or have-tos. It's about possibilities – the real possibilities we all have, however dire the situation, however bleak the outlook. It's also about choices. There are always choices. And given those choices you can opt for recovery and expanded horizons – or denial and shut-down. It's up to you.

You've already *made* a choice in buying this book. The next step is to read it. In doing so you may encounter occasional overlaps. That's because certain choices are interlinked. Instead of referring you back to an earlier chapter, some points may be re-stated. For immediacy and clarity, and because repetition is the mother of skill, the more you hear this stuff, the more likely you are to put it to good use.

Prologue

Let me say at the outset that I forgive my ex – and his new girlfriend – 100 per cent . . . for everything.

There, that's off my chest.

The truth is that, without them, I would not be where I am today: more happy, more content and more in control of my life than I have ever been.

If you'd told me I would be able to say this, and *mean* it, when I was first confronted with the fact that the man I'd been living with for twenty-five years had run off with a computer operator in her thirties, I would have laughed (hollowly) and gone on sticking pins in the wax effigies. Unknown to me, the 'relationship' had been on-going for two years and began on a skiing holiday which I'd given the man in question as a fiftieth birthday present.

At fifty-two, I suddenly found myself alone with a large mortgage (for which I was jointly and severally liable), a fourteen-year-old son (ditto), and no visible means of support. At that point I was so full of bitterness and bile, I could cheerfully have hired a hitman and disposed of the pair of them.

If you have recently been left in the lurch by some Lothario, you will know what I mean. 'Never,' I hear you cry. 'Never, never, never. I will *never* forgive the bum while I have breath in my body. And as for her . . .'

But here's the rub. Until you *do* forgive, until you let go of the resentment that is even now gnawing at your vitals, you won't be able to move on to the bigger and better future that lies ahead. Try to look at this as an opportunity rather than a disaster.

Naturally you feel hard done by. You *are* hard done by. But unless you can say, 'That's the past. It's over. This is now. Let's make sure nothing like it ever happens again,' then you won't be able to see the big picture. You will remain a victim. Not of fate, not of chance, but of your own entrenched attitudes.

Making sure that it never happens again doesn't mean never falling in love, never trusting, never forming another relationship. Making sure that it never happens again means taking responsibility for yourself and your life, becoming someone who is so secure in themselves that they can never be abandoned by anyone. Making sure that it never happens again means realizing that you are worth more than you have ever given yourself credit for and that, whatever anyone else thinks, you are fine – just as you are.

Refuse to let his memory waste any more of your precious time. Otherwise you are perpetuating his power over you. You're allowing him to influence your life, even though he isn't there any more. Do you want to give the rat that satisfaction?

That doesn't mean you don't need to grieve. You do. You've lost something which was once precious and you need to acknowledge that. The grieving process takes about two years and it's not easy. Sometimes it seems like one step forward and two back. But 'the longest journey begins with a single step' (Confucius), so the sooner you begin, the better.

Anything left after two years is just waste product or habit and should be ruthlessly sluiced away. Otherwise it will harden your arteries and corrode your spirit.

Being abandoned is like having someone you love die . . .

only more so. Don't get me wrong. I'm not trying to trivialize death. Far from it. But at least when someone you love dies, you can remember the wonderful times. Abandonment denies you even that small crumb of comfort. When a lover passes on, cherished memories help you over the trauma. When a lover leaves with another, what remains is angst and anger. Intimate remembrances of times past are overlaid by a black blanket of betrayal. Each waking thought, each nocturnal nightmare, is coloured by the knowledge that the person you loved is currently saying and doing the same things with *her* as he did with you. (I guarantee he's not inventive enough to write another screenplay.) So you can no longer picture the first time you held hands, made love, swore undying fealty, without having that image superimposed by an action replay, in glorious Technicolor, of him going through the same motions with someone new. Someone who has stolen your seat, undermined your confidence and left you feeling about as desirable as a dog's dinner.

It doesn't bear thinking about.

And yet you can't *stop* thinking about it. Round and round it goes like a CD stuck in a perpetual groove. Particularly in the small hours when you toss on your solitary couch and weep bitter tears into your pillow. She has him. And what are you left with? Nothing but rejection, red eyes and questions of the 'What could I have done? Where did I go wrong?' variety.

Add to all this negativity panic, despair, terror, disbelief, hope that it's all been a terrible mistake, and the conviction that nothing will ever be the same again.

Nothing *will* ever be the same again. But have you ever considered this: it could be *better*! It should be better. Because you deserve better than someone who treats you like a piece of used Kleenex.

Don't you? Well, *don't you*?

If your abandonment is recent, you may not believe it. Not yet. You may feel so low you aren't sure you deserve anything. You may be so panicked by the practicalities of getting through today that you haven't even had time to think about it. Hang on in there. The experience is a finite one. It doesn't go on for ever. Take it from one who knows: you'll get over it.

One word of warning. To *really* get over it and grow in the process, you need to learn the valuable lessons that are currently being thrust down your unwilling throat. If you behave like a headless chicken, if you moan, why me, why me, why me, if you leap into bed with the next available body, convinced that he, she or it is the answer to all your problems, then your future is just going to be a re-run of the horrible things you are experiencing right now. At the end of it all you'll be older, but no wiser.

To make sure that this *never* happens again, you must take charge of your own destiny. In order to learn and grow and change for the better – and ensure that any future relationships you embark on are undertaken from a position of want rather than need – you must first become your own best friend. That way, whatever happens in the future, you can never be totally abandoned again.

If you don't know where to start, be assured that you've already started by picking up this book.

There is an old Chinese curse: 'May you live in interesting times.' For me the last two years have been nothing if not interesting. I had to get very smart, very fast, or I wouldn't be here to tell the tale. I learned a lot about survival – mental, physical, spiritual and practical.

I also found out who my real friends were. Some people gave up on me almost immediately. As that social pariah, a manless woman, I was dropped from more dinner lists than the proverbial hot brick. Others didn't, even though I was bitter, obsessive, badly behaved, and burst into tears at the drop of a hat. A few people whom I hardly knew offered help and have since become firm friends.

The other thing I discovered was that abandonment is no respecter of age or class. From the single, childless career girl who may only have to reassemble her bruised ego, to the nineteen-year-old mother of two with the minimum of education and coping skills, to the middle-aged, middle-class mother like myself, caught in the poverty trap and widely considered to be unemployable and over the hill, abandonees are endemic in our society. Why? Because men can simply get away with it.

There is a growing army of 'abandoned women' out there – women left to pick up the pieces and cope with reality, to wrestle with the vagaries of a frequently unworkable and notoriously unsupportive social security system while their other halves go their merry way rejoicing. Abandoned women could form a political party if we weren't so busy trying to keep the wolf from the door.

My experience won't be your experience. But I'd like to pass on my own personal coping strategies. Also those gleaned from fellow travellers along the path of recovery. My hope is that this book will make your particular rite of passage less panic-stricken than mine has been.

And if I survived, so can you.

1 • Making a Drama out of a Crisis: Why Not?

In her marvellous book *Uncoupling: How and Why Relationships Fall Apart* Diane Vaughan has this to say: 'In order to uncouple, two people must disentangle not only their belongings but their identities.'

The second part of this equation is by far the most difficult to effect. It wasn't until I stopped automatically reading my other half's horoscope (Aries) alongside mine (Cancer) that I realized I'd at last laid my own particular ghost.

During the course of their time together, a couple builds up a corporate identity, a lovingly constructed tapestry celebrating their joined lives, which will vary in depth and richness depending on the length of the relationship and whether or not there are children involved. Time, effort, joy, love and shared experience are woven into this masterpiece, and it's impossible to simply divide it in two and get on with life when the relationship ends. To even begin to detach oneself from a mutually supportive situation, each thread must be painstakingly unpicked. To the abandonee, struggling to survive in a welter of betrayal, insecurity and lost love, the task may seem not only daunting but distasteful.

Is it any wonder, then, that many abandoned women behave badly, rending the tapestry like the Lady of Shallott and trampling it in fury under their feet?

Take the friend of mine who went round to the residence of her garden-proud ex-lover while he was 'otherwise engaged' upstairs and emptied all his decorative flower-pots into his ornamental pool. Or another who went to more extreme lengths and snuck by at dead of night to defecate on what she thought was an ornamental stone, only to discover next day that the stone had moved and she'd actually done the business on next door's unfortunate tortoise.

'Hit 'em where it hurts' seems to be the motto in this game of vigilante vengeance.

One particularly sartorial gent, who had foolishly omitted to get the keys back from his estranged wife, came home from the office one day to find the right trouser leg missing from every one of his Saville Row suits. Another, who had the temerity to call from Marbella, where he was holidaying with his new amour, to ask his ex to sell his Jaguar, discovered on his return a cheque for £25.00, the amount that she had advertised the car for in *Exchange and Mart*.

Finally there's the famous Lady Sally Moon, who denuded her philandering husband's priceless wine-cellar and delighted the village neighbours by depositing several bottles of his vintage plonk on their doorsteps alongside the morning milk. She then told the world about it in the popular press and on national TV, and has founded the Old Bags' Club for women such as herself who don't want to be nice and/or take abandonment lying down.

My own act of defiance was not exactly revenge, but it was very satisfying. I tore up every single pictorial reminder of our time together. This may sound childish, but it was a kind of ritual slaughter. Those snapshots represented our twenty-five years together and, in ripping and shredding the photo-albums and dumping them in the garbage, I effectively erased my ex-man from my existence. Like Monty Python's parrot, he had 'joined the choir invisible' and was 'no more'.

I only came to realize that, in destroying his memory, I

had also destroyed twenty-five years of my own life some two years later. By then I was able to acknowledge that the entire twenty-five years *hadn't* been a write-off. In fact the first fifteen had been pretty special. But at the time, the photo incident was what I needed to 'get me through the night'. It gave me a modicum of control over what had become an unbearable situation. It took me out of reaction into action. It also stopped me from doing anything more drastic.

Revenge is sweet, but it needs to be restrained or it can easily turn into spite. You have your liberty – and your karma – to consider. You don't want to land yourself in more trouble than you're in already. Or come back in the next life as a slug. In the throes of your righteous indignation try to steer clear of things that are self-destructive.

Things *not* to do

1. Pay the boys to come around and give him a good seeing to.

2. Beard the happy couple at the local pub and throw gin all over *her*.

3. Write threatening letters (evidence which can be used against you in court).

4. Make threatening or abusive phone calls (ditto).

5. Jump into bed with the nearest available body, even if you haven't had any sex for a long time. Sex does not equal love. If you're randy, try a bit of 'do it yourself'. As the old joke says, 'You'll meet a better class of person that way.'

6. Move house, unless you positively cannot afford to stay. A roof over your head represents security and for the

time being you need to keep as much as you can of your support system intact.

7. Alienate your mutual friends. Tell them your side of the story once, then drop the subject . . . if you don't want them to drop you. (See support system above.)
8. Post anything unmentionable through the letter-box.
9. Take to drink and mess up your head.
10. Take to chocolate-chip cookies and mess up your body.

On the other hand, this is not the time to give up smoking or take up jogging or forgo the occasional half of lager. Avoid anything, in essence, that involves will-power or adds extra stress for the time being. You need all your energy to cope with the immediate problems. The other things will wait until you're psychologically stronger. Meanwhile, be kind to yourself – if only to prove that *somebody* still loves you.

Things to do

1. Go to ground. When animals are hurt they crawl away into a corner and lick their wounds until they feel better. Don't rush headlong into a mad social whirl. (You should be so lucky if you're stuck at home with pre-school kids!) You're not ready for it yet.

2. Make a nest – with hot-water bottles and cushions and duvets and such – and *sleep*. As Shakespeare said, sleep 'knits up the ravelled sleeve of care'. It also gives you the energy to face whatever curve-balls life can throw at you and . . . it's *free*. If you have to get up early with the children, then go to bed when they do. If you find it impossible to sleep (which is often the case), try not to resort to pills which are addictive and also repress

REM (rapid eye movement) sleep which is the most refreshing cycle in your nightly dream-time. Try Horlicks or, if you don't like milk, chamomile tea. They both contain tryptophan, an amino-acid which soothes and calms.

NB Don't lie in bed allowing the whole thing to churn around and around. If you wake in the small hours, get up, make yourself your preferred drink and read (something soothing) until you feel like dropping off again. Or write down whatever is bothering you. Committing your thoughts to paper has the magical effect of flushing them out of your head. Then tear the paper into tiny pieces and flush it down the loo. Above all, don't worry if sleep eludes you. Depression notoriously interferes with sleep patterns. This is normal. It will pass. Meanwhile, learn to cat-nap to catch up.

3. Rearrange the furniture. Make the place look as different as possible from when *he* lived there. Give away his favourite armchair, mug, Black and Decker. Throw away that stuffed trout you always loathed. Clear out his clothes cupboard – and fumigate it – especially if he smoked, drank to excess or used strong aftershave. Redecorate the bedroom and turn it into your sanctuary with flowers and candles and romantic novels (free from the library) and whatever you fancy. Take the opportunity to stretch and spread. It's *your* space now . . . make the most of it.

4. After the first flurry of mad and justifiable reaction, take time to contemplate your life. Try not to make any hasty decisions. Your judgement will be impaired for some time. Coast. Cruise. Give your subconscious the benefit of the doubt. When you're ready to act, it'll let you know.

5. Talk it out – with your priest, counsellor, mother, best friend. Get it off your chest. Take any advice given with thanks and a pinch of salt. This is *your* life. No one else can live it for you.

6. Try not to be bitter. Hard, I know. But bitterness rebounds, pinches the face, stunts the soul. You may not be ready to forgive and forget. But try to forget at least.

7. Be your own therapist. Shout, scream, kick the cushions (not the cat). Letting off steam gets rid of excess bile and stops you moping.

8. Spring clean. Put your fury to some practical use. If you *do* eventually sell up and move on, you might as well get the best price you can for the place. If it's not your place, then a shiny new living space will reflect the shiny new you.

9. Write to old friends, preferably ones you may have lost touch with, who were in your life before you met your 'significant other'. This will remind you that you had a life before. A good life. And that you will have another one after. Much better.

10. Read romantic novels. Watch black-and-white movies. Listen to sad music. Not *your* song, of course. That's just masochistic. And *cry*. Crying is good. It's a natural reaction. Don't bottle up emotions. Let them out and they'll run their own course. Don't be surprised if you cry a lot. I used to find myself crying while I was driving and not even know I was doing it. Crying means you're getting better. It's when you can't cry that you're in trouble. Bottled up emotions have to come out somewhere and if they don't come out now, in the natural release of tears, they'll come out later on in something much worse, like a full-blown nervous breakdown.

I've said it already but it bears repeating: Don't get seriously involved with anyone on the rebound. Even if, at first sight, the person in question looks like the proverbial Knight in Shining Armour. On closer inspection he may turn out to be a dragon in disguise. Find yourself first. Entering another relationship before you've uncoupled from the first will just prolong the agony of real recovery.

Try to find solace in small things. A beautiful sunset, a child's smile. This may sound esoteric, but it's the emotional equivalent of looking after the pennies and allowing the pounds to look after themselves. Let yourself be moved – don't shut your heart away entirely. You'll need it again . . . when the hurt has healed.

If all else fails, remind yourself that there's a good side to everything. As Shirley Conran said in *Superwoman*, 'If your husband runs away with the au pair, at least you'll never have to watch *Match of the Day* again.'

2 • An Attitude of Gratitude

When someone walks out, our cosy, secure world is torn apart. We feel helpless, useless, clueless, gutless. Unable to take a decision, unwilling to make an effort, we are overwhelmed by the enormity, the injustice, of it all. This is disempowerment writ large.

Alone in an alien world, with no prop, no back-up, we veer between panic and despair, self-hate and outrage. Nothing, we are sure, will ever go right for us again.

To be told, at this time, to think positive, is enough to invite a punch in the mouth. But there *is* a way to regain control. The trick lies not in positive thinking but in positive focus.

Whatever you focus on, you attract.

If you focus on misery, despair, abandonment, that's what you'll experience.

If you focus on hope, happiness, new beginnings, that's where your reality will be.

You don't believe me? Try it.

No matter how dire the situation, it has a good side. There's always something, no matter how small, to which you can latch on to make you feel better.

Change your attitude and you can change your life. Because the truth is that it's not the situation which causes distress but your reaction to it. Some people thrive on long-haul flights, high-powered business meetings and living out of suitcases. Others have to be practically anaesthetized with

An Attitude of Gratitude

brandy before they can step on to a plane. Same experience, different perspectives.

The distinction between the two types lies in their focus. Type A focuses on enjoying the adventure, the miracle of flight. She looks forward to the movie, the view from the cabin as the sun sets, the champagne before dinner, the prospect of the successful meeting to come. Type B focuses on what might go wrong. She won't be happy until her feet are on solid ground again. She thinks that if God had wanted us to fly he would have given us wings, that there's six miles between her and the ground. Her mind scrabbles through action replays of all the plane crashes she's ever seen.

Type A is living in the present moment. Type B is caught up in some never-never land created by fear, which bears no relation to what is actually going on.

Which of these two types do you think is having a better time? One is excited and stimulated by challenge, the other is paralysed by problems that don't even exist. Challenges and problems. Same world. Different viewpoint.

You cannot control life. There are too many wild cards. What you *can* learn to do is control your reactions to it. Roll with the punches. Be open to change. Accept what you're handed as an opportunity to learn, grow and develop as a person in your own right.

Of course if you've been part of a pair for as long as you can remember, this will be like pulling teeth. The prospect of going it alone can be terrifying. But you can look at the situation in two different ways. Either as a familiar door slamming in your face, or as a brand new door opening to offer you a second chance to do all the things you couldn't do when you were cutting your cloth to suit someone else's jacket.

Which of these viewpoints best suits your needs?

Coping with rejection is hard. It's harder if you reject

yourself. Self-worth is the first thing that goes out the window when someone gives you the big E. Suddenly you are the wallflower at the party, the last kid to be picked for the team. Your mind begins to dredge up all the slights, the knock-backs and the put-downs that have ever happened to you in the past. Pretty soon it seems that nobody loves you, nobody has ever loved you, nobody will ever love you again.

Part of the lyrics of a famous sixties' song declared that if you couldn't be with the one you loved, you should love the one you were with. Well, the one you're with, more than any other, is you. So be gentle with yourself. Never lose in your head. And don't add guilt to misery. Give yourself the support you deserve. It's *not* your fault he left.

There'll be good days and bad days, of course. You're in a state of mourning, after all, for lost dreams as well as everything else. Don't be surprised if you burst into tears, get panicky, lose your temper. These are all natural reactions. What you can do to help yourself through the out-of-control period is to start to take control in small ways. Simple, undemanding coping strategies that will build up your self-worth and salve your bruised ego.

Here are a few to start you off:

1. Learn to relax. Taking a few minutes off every day to tune out and release tension can be very comforting. Schedule in your break as you would an important appointment. Some time when you know you won't be disturbed. Straight after the kids have gone to bed, or the minute you get home from work. Or, if all else fails, last thing at night. Take the phone off the hook. Put on your favourite music, lie down and let go. Consciously unwinding will calm you down and stop negative pressure building up. It will also help you sleep better.

2. If you find it impossible to relax because your mind keeps going over and over scenes you'd rather forget, **practise positive visualization**. (See Survival Strategy 2, p. 54.) Close your eyes and imagine a place where you've been very happy. Not somewhere you shared with the ex, obviously, but maybe a scene remembered from childhood when all the world was young and life was full of magic. A special, private place.

My own 'sanctuary' is a poolside high in the Andalusian mountains which has a spectacular view over the crescent-shaped bay of Malaga. Even in mid-summer, when the beaches are crammed to capacity, it is an oasis of tranquillity quiet enough to hear the cicadas sing. It belongs to friends who are kind enough to let me borrow it from time to time. Just writing about it makes me feel at peace.

Wherever you choose, try to recreate the scene in all its sensual detail. Is it light or dark, warm or cool? What are the colours, scents and sounds? Make it a place where no one can harm you. Think of it as surrounded by a white light which nothing bad can penetrate. Return to this place as often as you like. Allow it to calm and soothe you.

3. Indulge in a little self-talk – otherwise known as **affirmations**. Examples of these are anything from Emile Coué's famous, 'Every day in every way I'm getting better and better,' to, 'I like myself, I like myself, I like myself.' But anything you care to construct is acceptable as long as it assists in your own rehabilitation. 'I can cope.' 'I am strong and powerful.' 'Only the best is good enough for me.' Say them into the mirror with as much conviction as you can muster. Write them down and stick them where you can see them often during the day. On top of the word-processor. Above the sink. Carry them in your handbag. Use them as bookmarks.

Make sure they are positive, personal, non-judgemental affirmations and that they deal with you, not the other person. 'Who needs the bum anyway?' or, 'I'm better off without him,' will only focus you on your resentment and make you feel hard done by. 'I have a wonderful future' opens up all kinds of possibilities and helps you start the day in a positive frame of mind.

4. Try to smile. Smiling almost always gets a positive reaction. People smile back. They can't resist it. This will help you with your feelings of rejection and make their day better too.

Tony Robbins, the prolific American author, broadcaster and self-styled 'success coach', tells a story about a group of clinically depressed patients who were encouraged to smile for twenty minutes at a time as part of their therapy. During that time, even though they were only going through the motions, they found it impossible to feel bad. Soon they were smiling for real, not because they'd been told to. Robbins suggests that 'feeling follows action' rather than the other way around, that if you act as if you're happy, pretty, in control, soon you *will* be. It's worth a try. When we're really depressed we tend to affect a physical attitude which is hunched, slumped, almost foetal. The breathing becomes shallow, the energy level drops. The body is apeing the mind. If we reverse this, sit up, open our chests, get some air into our lungs we immediately feel better. Mind follows body. By taking physical control we regain mental equilibrium. We put ourselves back in the driving seat.

Of course real clinical depression needs medical intervention. If you feel you are dangerously low, don't be ashamed to ask for help. Shock can trigger ME, lower resistance to disease, even impair the immune system. And these days there is no longer a stigma about seeing a psychiatrist or therapist. Do it for those around you if not for yourself.

5. One sure-fire way to make you feel better almost immediately is to **stop taking in the news**. Cancel the papers. Turn off the TV at one minute to nine. The daily diet of doom and gloom dished out by the media is enough to bring even the most cheerful individual down. If you're upset to start with, you really don't need it.

This is not to suggest that you should become hard-boiled or uncaring, nor is it to denigrate the work done by certain investigative journalists into injustice, the state of the ozone layer and corruption in high places. But ask yourself this: do you want to have your emotions manipulated by a news editor at ITN?

If there is a riot going on in a council estate at the other end of the country, is that actually part of your truth? Now? In the moment? Is a gang of thugs throwing petrol bombs in *your* window? Or are you sitting quietly in your own home, safe and secure?

We are in danger of being turned into a nation of victims by TV moguls in pursuit of ratings. Don't allow this negative bombardment to trigger the kind of hormonal reaction appropriate to a real life-threatening situation when none exists.

Some old people are afraid to go out of their houses because they're terrified of being mugged. Their entire life experience has been curtailed and minimized because a small percentage of evil-doers have been given a large slice of publicity.

The truth is that we live in a wonderful, generous world. Most people would rather do you a favour than a bad turn. Most children are not abused. Most teenagers are kind, friendly, caring and responsible. Most politicians don't wear suspender belts while being beaten by madams in East Croydon. And 9,472,846 people *weren't* murdered today by a crazed serial killer.

Get things in perspective. Take back control. Turn off the telly. You'll feel better for it.

6. Finally, **try not to moan**. Moaning can become habit. As the centre of your own universe, you *can* control your focus. And out of your focus comes your experience.

A friend in need is a valuable commodity and unburdening yourself to someone close can be very comforting. But try not to abuse the privilege. It's your problem — sorry, challenge — and if you are still going on like a broken record six months after the split, don't be surprised if people you've known for years start to avoid you. Remember you need all the friends you can get, to expand your horizons, boost your social life and stop you ending up like Miss Havisham.

And now, a little exercise to re-frame your attitude.

Get two pieces of paper.

On the first make a list of all your ex's bad points, the things that used to drive you mad when he was about. His filthy habits. His thoughtlessness. The physical things about him that were less than a turn-on. Did he pick his nose, fart in bed, drop his dirty socks on the floor for you to pick up? Did he snore, drink, tell the same story over and over again at dinner parties and always forget the punchline? Did he leave a ring around the bath, smell, show you up in public and always forget your birthday? Get it all on paper.

On the second make a list of all the things you couldn't do when he was there. Be inventive. Make the possibilities BIG. If you secretly harboured a desire to spend time with Brad Pitt or travel to Timbuktu, say so. This list doesn't have to be grounded in reality. Dredge up those old dreams. Take them out of the airing cupboard and dust them off. Maybe

An Attitude of Gratitude

they'll work out this time around? If you've yearned to have your own florist shop, take a degree or be a company director, but your old man laughed you to scorn, *write it down*. There's no longer anyone to stand in the way of your ambitions.

Just you.

Scary, isn't it?

And exciting.

Now, take list one and read it through. Linger on each point with glee. Tell yourself what a lucky escape you had. Believe it.

When you've had enough laughs at his expense, tear the paper up into little pieces and flush them down the loo and, with them, your resentment.

Pick up list two and scan it. See what the future holds for you. Aren't you lucky? Ring one thing that you would truly like to accomplish, indulge in or attain. Never mind whether you can afford it or if it seems remotely possible. Take this list and stick it on your dressing-table mirror so that every time you look at it you get a pleasant glow of anticipation.

Allow yourself to be inspired.

Survival Strategy 1
How to Relax

Have you been so tense for so long that you wouldn't recognize relaxation if you met it in the street?

Check yourself out. Are you sitting comfortably? Or are you gritting your teeth, wrinkling your forehead, frowning? Are your shoulders hunched up round your ears? If so, did you realize you were doing any of these things?

Initially, you need to recognize the relaxation response. Then and only then can you learn to reproduce it.

Here's how.

Make a fist. Now squeeze your hand tight, tensing up your whole arm. Hold for a count of three – then let go. That relief you feel flooding through your arm is the relaxation response. Apply it to the rest of your body and you can teach yourself to relax in any situation. It's a simple skill but it produces powerful results. If your body is relaxed, your brain will be too. You'll make decisions from a position of tranquility rather than terror.

Below are some simple suggestions to get you started.

Begin by setting the scene. Choose a time when you know you won't be interrupted and take the phone off the hook. If it's daylight, draw the curtains. If it's night-time, turn off the lights. Put on your favourite music, something smoochy with a nice even rhythm, or you might want to buy one of the 'natural sound' relaxation tapes on the market (see Useful Addresses, p. 231). Lie down on the floor, with pillows arranged to support your head, feet and the small of your

How to Relax

back, and make yourself as comfortable as you can. Flat on your back with your arms by your sides, palms up, is best. But if you have problems with your lower back you may prefer to bring your knees up, keeping your feet flat on the floor. This neutralizes any arch behind the waist. It's up to you.

Now you're ready.

Close your eyes and clear your mind.

If this is easier said than done and your brain keeps hopping round like Jiminy Cricket, then focus on a calm, quiet memory. Alternatively, imagine you are on a desert island, lying on the beach. The sand is warm beneath your body. Run your fingers through the warm sand. Experience it. Feel the heat of the sun bathing your face in its golden glow. Imagine that a light breeze is blowing in from the sea, fanning your cheeks. Overhead the palm trees are swaying in a cloudless sky. The sound of the surf swishes soporifically in your ears and, from somewhere nearby, comes the desultory sound of gulls crying. Relax.

Start to breathe deeply. In through the nose. Out through the mouth.

Think about your toes. Are they tense? Give them a little wriggle and relax them. Relax your feet (if they're really relaxed they'll flop out to the side).

Relax your ankles, your calves, your knees and your thighs. Tighten up everything inside your pelvis – then relax – let it all go.

Now, starting at the base of your spine and working right up to the nape of your neck, imagine that each separate little vertebra is dropping down into the floor. Ease the hollow out behind your waist. Lengthen your back. Widen it. Now forget about it. Relax.

Take a deep breath in through your nose, fill your lungs with oxygen, lift your rib-cage up and out to the side. Hold the breath for a second then exhale in a great *whooooosh*, driving out all the tension with the stale air.

Begin breathing regularly again. In through the nose, out through the mouth. Focus your attention on your shoulders. If they're tight, ease them up to your ears, shake them out and relax them.

Relax the top of the arms and the elbows, the bottom of the arms and the wrists. Turn the hands palms upwards and allow the fingers to curl in lightly.

Finally, concentrate on the neck. If it's tense, and it may well be (the neck is one of the areas where tension collects with a vengeance), just release it by easing the head gently from side to side. Now centre the head. Feel the weight of it. It's enormously heavy. Twelve pounds or so. Imagine that weight falling slowly back through the floor to Australia.

Relax the jaw – let it drop open. Unclamp the tongue from the roof of your mouth. Relax the eyes – you were probably screwing them up without knowing it – and feel the cheeks softening out.

Draw your eyebrows up towards your hairline, then relax them and feel the tension draining away from the forehead and the scalp. Now imagine that your whole body is heavy and warm, sinking down through the floor. Relax.

With luck – and practice – you should now feel relaxed all over. Your body should feel heavy and warm. Lie there in this semi-somnolent state until the music comes to an end. Don't feel guilty. Wallow in it.

When you've had enough, get up – slowly. All your systems will have wound down and if you spring to your feet you may feel faint or dizzy. Take it gently. Roll over on to your right side, bring your knees into your chest, put your left hand down and gently ease yourself up into a sitting position. Now stand up. Take a few moments to breathe deeply before going about your daily business.

You should feel like a new person. Calm, confident, refreshed and ready to take on the world again.

If you have a tape recorder you might like to record the relaxation instructions so that you can talk yourself through them. Begin with the paragraph, 'Start to breathe deeply' and carry on to the end of the paragraph 'Draw your eyebrows up . . .', reading in a clear calm voice.

Whatever . . . enjoy the experience.

3 • Accentuate the Positive

The first thing you need to do when you find yourself in a state of abandonment is to count your blessings. This may sound like a *Mary Poppins* approach but it is a really effective way of getting things into perspective.

Living, as we do, in a free country with a health service which, even in its present dire state, is still the envy of most of the globe; with levels of sanitation and hygiene unknown in many Third World countries; with public transport and educational opportunities and free libraries; with TVs and labour-saving devices and running water in every home – we are millionaires compared with 90 per cent of the inhabitants of the planet.

Vast numbers of people live in war zones in daily fear of their lives. Free speech and the right to assembly may be unknown and ethnic cleansing the norm. In many places infant mortality is still rife and the average life expectancy no more than thirty years. Plagued by lice and internal parasites, whole groups of human beings literally don't know where their next meal is coming from.

We don't know how lucky we are. Nobody in Britain, to my knowledge, has to walk ten miles, barefoot, to get to school, or carry water an equal distance from the only unpolluted well in the area. But we hardly ever think of that.

There is a story about an Indian guru, passing through Heathrow Airport on a lecture tour. It was his first trip to Europe and he'd just arrived from the teeming slums of

Calcutta. He looked around the vast air-conditioned building, at the strip-lights and the shops and the restaurants, the conveyor belts and the rest-rooms and the smartly dressed uniformed personnel. Then he looked at the well-fed crowds, with their space-age luggage and their fashionable clothes, all hurrying and shoving and jostling to be first in line, faces pinched with anxiety and self-interest and ill-humour and he said, 'These people are living in paradise. I wonder if any of them realize it?'

Do you realize exactly how much you've got to be grateful for – in general, before you even start thinking about your own personal blessings?

If not, acknowledge it now. Make another list . . .

Focus on all the things you have going for you: not just what you own, but who you are, your strengths, support systems, pleasures. Even if it's just watching *Neighbours*. As long as it makes you feel good, write it down.

My blessings list reads like this:

1. *Son. Stevie. Fourteen at the time and in mid-GCEs. Having to be strong for him meant I couldn't be self-indulgent, drown my sorrows, fall apart at the seams or commit suicide, even though at some point I felt like doing all of these things.*

2. *House. Security. In joint names so I couldn't be kicked out. Built in 1826, granite, on three floors, fully furnished, vast kitchen, very beautiful. A source of joy. Double garage and garden. Nice area of town.*

3. *Flat in London. We had been renting it for twenty years so outgoings low. Again, nice area. Friend's son temporarily resident and covering utilities.*

4. *Family. Parents still living and in good health (as a last resort I could always go home). Daughter happily married and self-supporting.*

5. *Friends. Too numerous to mention.*

6. *Talents. Broadcasting, writing, teaching class.*

7. *Car. Paid for.*

8. *Savings. Not much but enough to keep wolf from door in the immediate moment.*

9. *Health and strength.*

10. *Support system. Doctor, accountant, hairdresser, lawyer, cleaning lady.*

11. *Clothes. Classic stuff so I didn't need to buy anything for at least three years. Also, in good times, had invested in cashmere and silk so I didn't look as though I was on my uppers when I went for interviews or meetings.*

12. *Books and paintings (nothing valuable in the disposable sense but a source of pleasure and comfort).*

13. *Records and tapes and videos (ditto).*

14. *Furniture, TVs, video recorders.*

15. *Word-processor, desk, filing cabinet, telephones, ansaphone.*

16. *Duvets, hot-water bottles, central heating, hot water, fridge, washing-machine and dryer.*

17. *Hair-dryer, heated rollers, make-up.*

18. *Good credit rating.*

So much for me.

Now make your own list. Take some time to write it out before you read on. Leave nothing out, however small. Enjoy the process.

Now, having fortified yourself with all the positive aspects of your life, it's time to grasp the nettle and thoroughly assess the nasty bits.

Be ruthless. Don't pretend things will sort themselves out,

Accentuate the Positive

do an impression of an ostrich or put the buff envelopes back in the post with 'not known at this address' written on them. Only when you confront the awful truth can you spare yourself the trauma of any more nasty shocks and begin to tackle the job in hand.

Where on the following scale of desperation does your particular scenario fit?

- Young, job, no kids.
- Young, job, kids.
- Young, no job, no kids.
- Young, no job, kids.
- Old, job, no kids.
- Old, job, kids.
- Old, no job, no kids.
- Old, no job, kids.

Naturally there are all sorts of variations in between. Each situation carries its own set of challenges.

If you're young with a job and no kids, your task will be the least difficult. You'll need to find somewhere to live, split the communal property and rebuild your self-esteem. Of course, one can't generalize and recovery may not be so simple if you have to deal with negative equity, and a louse who stripped the communal home down to the light bulbs before running off with your mother. But at least you have no dependants, there's money coming in and you have your whole life ahead of you. You'll have to adjust to not having a man around the house but your relationship probably won't have been going long enough to accumulate too many mutual possessions or for the pair of you to have become joined at the hip. As the old song says, you can 'pick yourself up, dust yourself off and start all over again'.

One rung down comes young with a job and kids. This brings in the extra dimension of where to find baby-sitters and time alone, physical exhaustion and the strain of being a one-parent family.

Lower still is young with no job and kids. Money problems and isolation really loom large here. Social security won't keep you in a manner to which anyone should have to become accustomed and you have the added restrictions of no social life. But there *are* jobs out there provided you can organize the practicalities of child-minding and overcome the terror of getting back into the job-market. With youth and health on your side, the sky is truly the limit.

Then there's old with a job and no kids. I'm not being ageist here. For old, read thirty plus. Genetically we are classified as 'ageing primates' after that. In this instance the relationship has probably been going on for some time so the bonds will be harder to sever. Assuming your partner was also working, you will have had a decent standard of living below which, with only one income, you will have to drop. Living space will be smaller, disposable income less and the holidays abroad may have to go. But at least you *have* an income. There is also another dimension to your life, since presumably you have friends in the workplace. The chances of meeting someone new are less than they were when you were in your mid-twenties but you're not totally isolated.

To the category old with job and kids add the problems of coping with teenage traumas as well as your own. However, when they're not dealing with the angst of puberty, teenagers can be tremendously supportive, ruthlessly realistic and great fun. They can also give you a positive answer to the question, 'What have I got to show for the last twenty years of my life?' They don't need ferrying to and from school any more and they can get part-time jobs if money is really tight.

Accentuate the Positive

Worst of all possible worlds is the category in which I found myself: old – well, mature – with no job and a teenage son. This can be a tough one – especially if your ex is unwilling or unable to provide financial support. Every day brings another bill and you have to confront the distinct possibility that you may never be in another relationship again.

This, then, was my liability list:

1. *Mortgage. Vast. Soon after I took over the payments (our deal had been: he paid for the house, I covered the flat), I received a solicitor's letter to say that my partner had been defaulting on the mortgage for some time. The building society was about to foreclose and repossess the house. As I was self-employed and fifty-two, the society wouldn't accept me as sole mortgagee. I couldn't sell without the ex-partner's permission. And the bottom had just dropped out of the property market. Catch 22.*

2. *Flat. Shortly after I took over the mortgage the tenant in London moved out leaving me with another set of bills to pay.*

3. *Family. Miles away. Me in Scotland, them in Wales.*

4. *No financial security. I was self-employed, making a good second income in the fitness field which was enough to pay for extras but certainly wouldn't cover the basics. Even this fizzled out in the six months following my abandonment – the exercise bubble finally burst, but also I was so obsessed with my own problems I was no longer able to be supportive to other people and so lost most of my clients. I was so busy trying to keep my head above water on a daily basis that my inspiration and my other source of revenue, writing, dried up altogether.*

5. *Savings. I was caught in the poverty trap of having just enough savings to disqualify me from help with the mortgage*

or any form of social security. As a self-employed person, I couldn't get dole anyway (though I still had to pay National Insurance) so what I ended up with was an extra six pounds a week on my family allowance as a single parent. Twenty years' worth of savings went in just under twelve months. On the bread-line, I was still living beyond my means.

6. *Age.* Fifty-two. Visiting a government careers office to ask about retraining and volunteering to go back to university (I'd gained an entrance to Aberdeen to do a part-time English degree), I was told that if I wanted to do that for my own amusement, fine, but I should realize that by the time I qualified I would be fifty-six and (I quote) unemployable. It was suggested that I might like to get a job stacking shelves in the local supermarket. The hourly rate wouldn't have covered the mortgage let alone the utilities, food, etc. Very inspiring! Luckily the interview made me so mad it motivated me to prove the short-sighted individual who conducted it totally wrong. And I have, although I didn't take up the university place. Plenty of time for that when I'm seventy-two and looking for something to fill up my day.

7. *Angst.* For a person who has always considered herself a pretty tough cookie, I was horrified at how badly I reacted to the betrayal. It wouldn't be too much of an exaggeration to say that I was devastated, wiped out, floored. My brain fogged up, my reactions slowed down and I became desperately accident-prone. The slightest thing drove me to despair or rage. I shouldn't have been allowed to drive, or operate a gas-oven or use the scissors. My judgement went to pot. And so did I. All this, even though I should have rushed up to the woman in question, flung my arms around her and thanked her for taking the man off my hands. Go figure.

Now make your list.

Accentuate the Positive

Once you have it in black and white, this is the worst it can get. From now on, there's only one way to go: up.

First, take an overview. Like me, you'll probably find that some assets also figure in your liability list. Here is where you begin to exercise your power of choice. If they are more of a liability than an asset, then it may be time to get rid of them. If they are more of an asset, then you can choose to deal with the liability aspect or at least stop moaning about it.

For instance, I decided to view my house as an asset rather than a liability. It offered security and a certain standard of living that I was unwilling to relinquish at that particular time. I took an executive decision to stay where I was until my son had finished his secondary education and then sell up and move back to London. Once I'd made the choice and stopped feeling trapped, solutions presented themselves in short order. The house's size and central location allowed me to let half the double garage to a solicitor's office round the corner and take in lodgers from the local theatre. I had to lose a certain amount of privacy but my home, in effect, began to pay for itself.

I also found out, when putting my blessings and liabilities down on paper, that my asset list was twice as long as my debit one. This had the effect of cheering me up immediately.

I hope yours is the same. If it isn't, don't despair. Getting your priorities in order could just alter your whole point of view.

4 • Priorities

An acquaintance of mine had a mother who saved bits of string and brown paper. She put the string in a drawer (in case she might need it) and the brown paper behind the Welsh dresser (in case it might come in handy). This went on for twenty years, with layer upon layer of paper pushing the piece of furniture more and more off balance. Eventually, the inevitable day came when a final piece of paper, wafer thin though it was, pushed the whole thing down on top of her. She was hospitalized with a broken collar-bone and severe bruising. And all because she didn't want to throw away a piece of brown paper.

Women are often hoarders underneath. We hang on to clothes, ideas and men well after their sell-by date. Attics and cellars country-wide are stuffed to bursting point with things people don't really want but which they are afraid (yes, *afraid*) to throw out, in case...

In case of what? Fire, theft, flood, the new one might break down, winkle-pickers might come back into fashion? Not in your lifetime, baby.

Yet it's only by clearing the clutter out of your heart, your head and your hall cupboard that you make space for wonderful, new, exciting things to fill the gap. Fate has already relieved you of one of those outmoded items (namely your man), and presented you with the perfect opportunity to review the rest of the dross lurking in your life. Make the most of it.

Here's your chance to get your head together, to streamline your existence, to find out what you really need to make you happy and what you've been persuaded you need by other people. Forget television commercials or what the neighbours have or peer pressure. You are an individual. Here's where you find out the difference between a wish and a want. Here's where you choose what to jettison and what to retain. You are not what you own.

So let's get started. More lists!

What You Need (really need)

- A roof over your head.
- A car: if you already have one; if you need to travel long distances to work; if you have to ferry small children to and from school; if you have to collect loads of shopping.
- Food.
- Clothing.
- One luxury. For the good of the spirit and so that you don't feel wholly deprived. This can be as frivolous as you wish: A monthly massage, a weekly tea-dance down the palais, a regular trip to the movies or the theatre, fags (tut-tut), whatever helps you through the night and doesn't break the bank.

My luxury was my cleaning lady, Eileen, who came in for three hours a week and cost fifteen pounds. Wonderful Eileen, unruffled and down to earth. Not only did she change the sheets and scrub the bath, she did all those other things that I always meant to get around to but never did, like cleaning the oven and removing mouldy bits from the back of the fridge before they mutated into something dangerous. And taking down the curtains and washing them, without even being asked! I taught an extra exercise class solely to pay her wages but it was worth every minute and every penny.

This surprisingly short list was all I could say with my hand on my heart that I really *needed* to get by.

What You Don't Need (even if you want it)

- A car – if you live in a large town with a good transport system. Think of road rage and traffic jams and the hassle of finding parking. Who needs it? In London it is faster to go by tube, so you save time. And when you add up the cost of road tax, insurance, petrol, repairs, car-wash and depreciation, by selling or not owning a car you also save money. Quite a bit of it. Other pluses: It's better for your waistline to walk; better for your heart and the ozone layer to cycle. If the only thing you use the car for is shopping, work out the cost of the annual outlay on your four-wheeled friend and you'll find that it's cheaper to take a taxi to the supermarket. Some hypermarkets even run a free bus service. If all you need the car for is to take the kids to school, maybe a neighbour with children at the same school might give them a lift in exchange for petrol money or baby-sitting.

- Cable TV – Even if *all* your kids' friends have it. Let them go watch it elsewhere. It'll give you five minutes peace!

- The very latest model anything. If the old CD player works you don't need to replace it. Not at the moment, anyway.

- Named brands of anything. With clothes you are giving the company free advertising, with food you are paying for smart packaging. Do you really want some PR whizz-kid buying a yacht at your expense?
- Anything belonging to *him*. Chuck it away.
- Clothes that have been hanging in the wardrobe for ten years. Even if they come back into style, your face will have outgrown them.
- Papers/milk delivered – unless you are very old, very isolated, in love with the milkman or this is your chosen luxury.
- A mobile phone.

What Can You Put Up With or Do Without (for the time being)?

In my case I chose to put up with staying where I was for three years to allow my son to finish his schooling. Also, since suitable candidates were thin on the ground and my disposable income was zero, I decided I could do without a bloke, a social life, new clothes and treats until finances improved. If this sounds Spartan, remember it was my choice. I'm not martyr material. And in practice it wasn't so bad. When I *did* get an occasional windfall, like when my dad sent me a tenner for my birthday and we got a take-away pizza, it tasted better than any meal eaten at one of the best restaurants in more affluent and blasé days. One thing about being short of funds, it really makes you appreciate things when you get them.

What Can You Not Put Up With or Do Without (under any circumstances)?

My list:

- *The flat in London. I needed somewhere to go after my three years were up. The solution was to let it meanwhile.*
- *Eileen. For reasons already mentioned.*
- *Car. I needed it to transport my sound system and weights and such to my workplace, a leisure centre six miles out of town.*
- *Hair colour. An expense, but having been blonde for thirty years I wasn't prepared to let such a major part of my identity go down the tubes. And whether or not it's true that blondes have more fun, fun at the time was so thin on the ground, I figured I needed all the help I could get.*

What are You Willing to Invest to Make Things Better (now and in the long run)?

An important item this and one on which your future happiness could depend. The universe is on your side but the world doesn't owe you a living. And investment does not necessarily involve money. Two much more valuable commodities are time and effort. Investment of time and effort can improve your job prospects and open up your social, spiritual and romantic possibilities.

Work. Nobody's going to ring out of the blue and say, 'You're exactly the person we've been looking for.' That only happens in Meg Ryan movies. Put yourself about. If you're in work but because of your changed circumstances you want or need a better position, more money, promotion – ask. People are not mind-readers. Let them know the score. Network. Be seen around. If you haven't got a job but desperately need one, don't be proud. Get out your little black book and ring everyone you knew when you were working. Let them know you're available. And don't wait for the perfect job to come along. Bringing some money, any money, in is a great boost to the self-esteem. And it opens up the floodgates of abundance. Pop down to your local job centre and look on the boards (don't hang around – it can be very depressing), go to the library and scan the situations-vacant columns. Look at personnel-wanted ads in your local newsagent's window. If it's hard to commit yourself to full-time work because of small children, consider part-time. If you haven't worked for ages (or if you've never worked) and are nervous about starting, consider something temporary. Around Christmas and sale times, for instance, most stores are looking for temporary staff. It's a good way to ease yourself into the job market, and to find out whether selling is your *métier*. And who knows, if you're good at it and they like you, a temporary fill-in may blossom into a full-time post.

Social. Call all your friends – not to bitch but to say that you are in a position to make up numbers at dinner parties. Or how about a job in a bar? That way you'll have money coming in, the atmosphere of a social life without having to pay for it, you'll meet new blokes and, since a lot of them will be wanting to tell you *their* troubles, you won't feel so bad about your own.

Spiritual. A life crisis is a wonderful opportunity to contemplate one's place in the scheme of things, to step off the treadmill and take stock. One of the reasons religion has outlasted so much bad press is that it can be a great comfort in times of trouble. If you already have a faith but have let your involvement lapse, this may be a good time to rejoin your Church. If organized religion is anathema to you, there are plenty of spiritual alternatives: Buddhism, Rastafarianism or the Gaia principle that we are all connected and one with the universe. Reading self-help books is a good beginning. For me, Frederick Bailes' *Hidden Power for Human Problems* changed the way I looked at my life and, ultimately, my life experience. You'll find lots of suggestions in the recommended reading section on pp. 229–30. If you're a paid-up agnostic, you might like to test the water with a yoga class (see Survival Strategy 7). Yoga is not a religion, more a meditation in movement which puts one in touch with universal principles through physical discipline, breathing techniques and mental equilibrium.

Romantic. You might prefer to put this area of your life on hold until you get everything else straightened out. Why not? You may not be ready for a new man yet. You may never be ready. But be assured that if and when you are ready, there are men around. See Chapter 13 on how to meet some.

Finally, a word about **money**. If you *do* have any to invest, then don't hoard it. Get it out there where it'll do you some good. Speculate to accumulate. Use it for whatever you think will give you the edge, whether it be re-training, buying a franchise or having a face-lift.

Now it's your turn to compile your lists:

1. What you need (a want).

2. What you don't need (a wish).

3. What you can put up with or do without (until you get your head together: never put up with anything for any longer than is absolutely necessary).

4. What you cannot put up with or do without (under any circumstances).

5. What effort you are willing to invest to make things better (now – a change of attitude doesn't cost anything – and in the long term – if you want to write a bestselling novel or an Oscar-winning screen-play, how many hours a day are you willing to invest until it's done?).

Review your lists and consider how you can start to act on them. Remember, you do have choices. And *you* are in charge.

Survival Strategy 2
Creative Visualization

Creative visualization is a way of harnessing the power of your imagination. It can be an effective form of daydreaming, or a tool to snap you out of the negative and into a state of positive energy.

It may seem fanciful to conjure up a picture of your heart's desire in your head and then expect to get it. But thoughts are powerful things. So powerful that in their negative guises of stress, worry, and fear they can produce real physical manifestations such as ulcers, hypertension and cancer. Why, then, in their positive form of joy, appreciation and the expectation of abundance should they not change our life for the better?

Creative visualization, sometimes referred to as creative imagery, works on the premise that the subconscious mind believes anything it's told – which is why stage hypnotists can induce people to eat onions as though they were apples and dance like John Travolta when they have two left feet. Hypnotic trance is an extreme form of relaxation in which the subconscious is particularly susceptible to suggestion – a twilight state, similar to that experienced between sleeping and waking. For this reason, the optimum times to practise creative visualization are first thing in the morning, just as you're coming round, or last thing at night, just before you drop off. However, if you use the techniques outlined in Survival Strategy 1, How to Relax, to get you into an appropriately receptive mood, it can be effective any time.

Having wound yourself down to a pleasant state of drowsiness (and with practice this shouldn't take more than a couple of minutes), you simply form a picture in your mind of what you would like to have: a new home, a better body, an exciting job, a sensational lover, excellent health. The choice is yours. The subconscious mind, having accepted the picture as truth, will then find a way to make the dream reality.

The trick is not to worry about ways and means, just to visualize the situation complete and then let it go. Once, when I needed some money for the gas bill and couldn't work out where it could possibly come from, I got a totally unexpected tax rebate for almost the exact amount.

It helps if you make your visualization as detailed as possible. Use all your senses to persuade the subconscious that the picture you are sending it is a true one. Smell the roses. Feel the wind in your hair. Touch the velvet. See the sunset. Hear the bird song. Taste the champagne. Imagine the whole thing as a movie, with you as writer, director and star. Practise daily. Enjoy yourself.

The final challenge comes with the leap of faith. For creative visualization to be effective, you must believe that it *can* happen. You must believe that the universe is an abundant and nurturing place which wishes you only good. Believe that you deserve that good. Then sit back and wait for the good to manifest itself in its own good time.

Sometimes results are instantaneous (like my tax rebate). More often they unfold slowly like the petals of a flower. Be patient. Plant the seed, water it with daily visualization and, eventually, you'll have a tomato plant, or a rose bush, or an old oak tree with yellow ribbons round it.

Keep your mind open to possibilities; be prepared for answers to come from unexpected directions. I had always wanted a place in the sun but hadn't the financial wherewithal. A few weeks after starting to visualize it, some friends who had been living in Spain returned to Scotland and offered me free use of their luxury flat in Malaga so that I could complete the book I was writing. Thanks to their generosity, I can use it whenever they aren't in residence. I got my own place in the sun without the outlay or the financial upkeep – the best of all possible worlds. You don't have to own something to enjoy it.

If things don't happen straight away, don't give up in disgust. Persistence pays off, as does patience. We live in an age of instant gratification. But the universe has its own timescale; it cannot be hurried, hassled or coerced.

Never try to use creative visualization to wish another ill. We are not practising black magic here. Certain cosmic laws apply and that kind of malpractice has a way of rebounding on the practitioner.

If you are still sceptical about the power of imagination to change your reality, try the following test:

Sit in a chair and clear your mind.

Close your eyes and breathe regularly – in through the nose, out through the mouth, counting backwards from ten to one.

As you count, imagine that you are walking down a flight of ten steps.

With each step you are becoming more relaxed.

When you get to the bottom step you find a lemon and a knife.

Sit on the step, pick up the lemon and cut it in half with the knife.

Now take one half of the lemon and sink your teeth into it.

What are your reactions? Has your mouth filled with saliva? Are your lips puckering with the tartness of the fruit?

And this is just a pretend lemon!

Yet it has produced a definite physiological effect.

Put the lemon in the pretend litter-bin and the knife in your back pocket. Now count yourself back up the steps from one to ten.

Open your eyes.

Welcome back.

According to José Silva's *The Silva Mind Control Method*, the three prerequisites for effective creative visualization are desire, belief and expectation.

Desire. Often we think we want something when in actual fact we don't *really* want it. There is a difference between real, true, overwhelming desire and something which just seems like a good idea. So be sure you've thought the whole thing through. Say you want a new lover, handsome, strong and rich. Would you still want him if he beat you, cheated on you and was so vain you could never get into the bathroom? If not, better add gentle, faithful and considerate to the equation. Be specific.

Belief. Give your dreams free rein but remember that your subconscious is more likely to accept a goal which is grounded in possibility. If you live in the Balls Pond Road you are unlikely to bump into Tom Cruise in your local Asda. Apart from that, TC is currently married to Nicole Kidman (true happiness can't be bought at someone else's expense) and, even if he wasn't, can you believe it possible he is likely to fall in love with you make-up-less, wearing your old track suit, entangled with a trollyload of fish fingers and in possession of a screaming toddler? If not, try something you feel is more likely.

Expectation. This is all about self-esteem. If you're suffering from a surfeit of unworthiness, an occupational hazard if you've just been traded in for a new model, then deep down you may not feel you deserve what you want. You may covet your goal desperately, believe that it is achievable, but still not expect it to materialize because 'good things never happen to me'. Lack of self-esteem can put a serious spanner in the imaging works. A little self-talk can work wonders in this department. Sit yourself down in front of the dressing-table mirror, stare yourself straight in the eye and say, 'I am a valuable human being. My opinions, my dreams, my needs, my desires are as valid as anyone else's. I am a special person. I deserve the best the universe has to offer.'

Then take a deep breath and get on with it. Here's how:

1. Decide what it is that you want. One thing at a time – let's not confuse the issue.

2. Find a quiet spot, at a quiet time, phone off the hook, make yourself comfortable, close your eyes and relax.

3. Visualize your goal with as much clarity and feeling as you can. Dress the set. Light it. Add colours. Props. Flowers. A full-scale orchestra with Pavarotti if it helps the atmosphere. Picture the whole scenario as happening here and now, not in the unforeseeable future. Savour it.

4. After the session, unwind slowly. Stretch like a cat does when it wakes. Smile in anticipation of the actuality to come. Wheels have been set in motion.

5. Focus on your goal often. Allow it to drift into your mind at any time. While you're doing the dishes, changing the baby, standing in the check-out queue, lazing in the bath, sitting on a rush-hour bus. Savour it. Listen to hints that seem to come from nowhere as to how the object of your desire might be achieved. Act on them. See where they lead. It's like a cosmic treasure hunt.

6. Suspend your disbelief as you would at a movie or a

pantomime. Don't allow doubts to creep in. Normal rules do not apply here. You are creating a new reality.

7. Give yourself a pat on the back. When you've achieved your goal (note I don't say 'if'), acknowledge it. Allow yourself credit for a job well done, for the time and effort and positive belief you've put into bringing your vision to fruition. Don't say it was a fluke, or coincidence or that it would have happened anyway. You are extending your horizons, entering into possession of an untapped energy that has been dormant for far too long. Congratulations are in order.

When you first begin to practise this new skill, you may find that all your fears and concerns surface to crowd out your new positive programming. Especially during those times (early morning and late at night) recommended for imaging. When the mind is overwhelmed by worry or despair, it can simply go into overdrive. In this instance, don't try to blot out the thoughts, they'll only surface again. Remind yourself that they are *just* thoughts, with no power to hurt you unless you let them. Allow them to pass through your head without hindrance until you're a little more in tune. Use creative visualization in conjunction with relaxation (see p. 34) as a way to centre yourself, calm the mind, release tension and open a mental doorway through which you can move into untroubled sleep or step confidently into a more positive day. Gradually you will get to the point where you feel strong enough to practise imaging proper.

Everything around you, from the chair in which you're sitting to the cup from which you're drinking your coffee, began as an idea in someone's head. That's the process: thought leads, reality follows.

We are all creating reality all the time. At this moment, writing this book, I am creating a dialogue with you, the reader. Outside, it is a bleak December day, with traffic in snarls and frantic shoppers hurling themselves like lemmings through crowded stores in search of last-minute Christmas presents. Inside I am curled up cosy in bed, warm and secure, putting thoughts on paper which you are reading in the form of words. With this act we have bridged time and space. Your time and space is different from mine. And yet we are joined. We are one. In this moment. In this thought. Whether your reality is next door and tomorrow or ten years hence at the other end of the world.

This is incredible magic. And we are incredible beings to be able to work such a miracle.

And since I have your attention, know this, whoever and wherever you are: I wish you well. I wish you joy and peace and love, learning and growing and happiness and freedom from pain.

Know that, however deserted or miserable or lonely you may feel at this moment – it will pass. I've been there, maybe that's *why* I've been there? So I could write this book?

It's a thought.

Thoughts are powerful beyond belief. They can change the world. For better or worse. Why not make it better?

Direct your thoughts to visualize a better future.

Give it your best shot. It's your future, your reality.

What have you got to lose?

5 • All the Things You Are

There are two types of security: material (external) and psychological (internal). The first comes from having shelter and sustenance, the second comes from the knowledge that you are a valuable human being in your own right.

When someone leaves you for someone else, it can feel as though they've taken a hatchet and cut you down the centre. Only half of you is left. And that half must be useless, mustn't it? Otherwise why would the other person have left in the first place? The loss of material security can be difficult to deal with. The loss of identity, credibility, self-worth cuts to your very heart.

It's a wound that no amount of money or success can cover up. It needs to be dealt with from the inside out.

At the moment you may feel like a frightened rabbit, an abject failure, an emotional wreck, but in fact you are the you you've always been. You may have lost part of yourself along the way but you are still a whole person. And a much better person than you are currently giving yourself credit for. And as soon as you find out who that person really is, you'll be well on the way to recovery.

No matter how pressing your problems, you need to get this one right before you go any further. Because if you don't know who you are, how can you know what you want?

If you moved from the parental home directly to the marital one without any break, this may be the first time you've had a chance to be yourself, not what someone else expects you to be.

So take time out to reflect:

Do you like yourself?

If not, how do you expect anyone else to?

If not, why not?

Are you a bad person?

Or have you just been programmed to believe you are?

When we are little, playing happily with our toys, are we constantly praised for being good? No, we're left to our own devices while our mother gets on with the housework, the cooking or talking to her friend on the phone. But should we accidentally break something... plenty of feed-back then: Naughty. Bad girl. Now look what you've done. How many times have I told you not to...?

In the first couple of years of our life the word we probably hear most is 'No'. Naturally we need to be taught not to stick our fingers in the light socket or hurl ourselves off the top of the wardrobe, but a lot of the noes are to do with other people's comfort, not ours. And girls, especially, are still expected to be nice, defer to others, conform, or, as in my case, not show off. This constant barrage of negativity can have a profound effect on a young mind. It can sink deep into the psyche leaving a feeling of worthlessness and inadequacy that is hard to eradicate in later life.

Being left in the lurch is guaranteed to bring all these feelings to the fore. But that's all they are: feelings. They aren't the *truth*.

The truth is that you are a unique human being, no better or worse than anyone else. You make mistakes. Everybody does. If you look on these mistakes as a warning signal never to try anything new, you'll have a very boring life. If you view them as a learning curve, you will constantly grow and change and experience and... live to be happy.

In the self-help workshops which I run we begin with the following exercise:

Participants sit in a circle and one by one take a few minutes to explain to the rest of the group who they are. Most people find this extraordinarily difficult. Quite simply, they *hate* it. Talking about themselves makes them feel vulnerable, exposed, naked almost. They tend to down-grade themselves (what is it about the British that they consider saying something good about themselves the eighth deadly sin?) and they don't talk about who they *are* – for instance, 'I am a dependable friend' – but about what they do – 'I am a computer operator'. Some people blush or stammer. Some stop after their name and their occupation. They've never thought of themselves in any other context. Almost everybody heaves a huge sigh of relief when it's over.

But the saddest participants of all are those who say, 'My name is Jemima Bloggs and my problem is . . .'

You are not your problems. You are not your job. You are not what you own.

So what are you?

You are many, many things. Teacher and pupil, mother and daughter, lover and friend, neighbour, nurturer, gardener, creator, cook, traveller, seeker after truth. You can be all or any of these things. You are as unique as a snowflake. To put yourself in a box that says 'typist', 'housewife' or even 'company director' is to lose sight of the truly diverse and amazingly versatile creature that is you.

Most people never think about who they really are. They live their lives being what other people want them to be and then wonder why they feel short-changed. The bitterness and frustration born of sublimating your true self to the desires of others can manifest itself physically in problems such as arthritis and ulcers. We've already said you shouldn't take your happiness at other people's expense, but then neither should they be able to take their happiness at yours. You are not a doormat.

Take time now to penetrate the crust of conditioning and recognize all the wonderful things that are contained within your skin. You'll be pleasantly surprised.

By doing this exercise in the comfort of your own home, you are at least spared the embarrassment of exposing yourself to a roomful of strangers. Here's your chance to find out who you are without worrying about other people's opinions. No one is going to judge you. And please don't judge yourself. Be honest but keep an open mind. It's just you and a piece of paper.

Take a pencil now and make a list of all the things you are. Don't take anything for granted. Even something as simple as cooking a pancake takes skill and co-ordination. Are you a swimmer, painter, mother, ballroom dancer? You don't have to be a geo-physicist or the prime minister to be special. Whatever you are makes you special – get it all down.

There are a couple of rules:

1. Make it subjective. Each line should begin with, 'I am . . .' So, 'I am a gardener' rather than 'I like gardening.' The latter is doing rather than being. Even better, 'I am a successful, green-fingered gardener.' Allow yourself to savour the power of praise. Acknowledgement is not vanity. Even if you've spent your life being criticized by other people, you never have to criticize yourself. Which brings us to rule number two . . .

2. Don't add negatives to your list. For instance, you may have written, 'I am a mother.' If you are guilt-ridden (aren't we all?) about all the things you could have done better when bringing up your children, don't write, 'I am an indifferent mother.' In whose eyes? None of us is perfect. To try for perfection is to set yourself up for failure. This doesn't mean you should drop your standards – by all means aim for excellence. Excellence is an attainable goal.

Take at least fifteen minutes now to brainstorm all the things you are. Make the list as long as you can. Leave out nothing. Make it *positive*. Give it a bit of pizazz. 'Nurturer extraordinaire' sounds better than 'chief cook and bottle-washer'. Pin it on the mirror and read it aloud with feeling.

You'll be amazed at how exceptional you are. Think of all the people who are touched by what you do, whose lives are enriched by knowing you. Even if they don't appreciate it. Appreciate yourself! You are a very special human being. The world would be a much poorer place without you.

This exercise alone should prove how much you are worth. Right now. When you learn a new skill, add it on. It won't be long until you need a bigger piece of paper. Next time someone (perhaps yourself) tries to put you down, think of your list, smile sweetly and ignore them.

As a final flourish, choose two words from your list that sum you up. These could be anything from 'powerful communicator' to 'inspirational dreamer' to 'good friend'. Make the essence of these two words as close to what you've discovered about yourself as you can.

At the top of the page write your name, 'I am Jane Doe' followed by your two special words: 'wonderful person'.

And never let anyone tell you any different.

6 • I Thought as Much!

Some of the richest people in the world are also the most miserable. Having so much, they are consumed by the fear of losing it. No amount of money will give them security. They will always want more. Unless they change their thinking. In contrast some of the poorest people in the world, Buddhist monks for instance, are also the most content. They have an inner security – an abundance mentality – which no amount of money can buy. They trust in the universe to provide what they need – and, lo and behold, it does.

Think misery, poverty, hopelessness and your life reflects it, no matter how much you have squirrelled away in a Swiss bank account. Expect joy, abundance, enjoyment, and you're much more likely to get it.

Thoughts are things and what you think attracts what you manifest . . . for good or ill.

When you're abandoned by someone you love and trust it's tempting to think in black and white. 'It's all their fault. I'm totally innocent. They deserve to be punished.' But, no matter how abominably your ex has treated you, there must have been shades of grey in there. When you can begin to acknowledge this, you'll be on the road to recovery. Until you can acknowledge this you will be stuck in a rut. Only when you stop blaming can you start growing.

We all know people who, having been treated badly, are still talking about it twenty years later. The incident, what-

I Thought as Much!

ever it was, has left them bitter. It has coloured their whole life – for the worse. Who has done this terrible thing to them? They have.

We also know people who have been devastated by some unfair situation but who have used it to rethink their future and create something better. Who has done this wonderful thing for them? They have.

Their histories might be identical. The difference in results comes purely from the difference in thinking. The person living in the past is still being controlled by the one who let them down. The other has been able to let go – and move on to a more compelling future.

You don't have to *like* what's been done to you. You'd need to be a saint or a masochist for that. However, you can call a halt to the 'poor me, you're to blame' cycle by declaring it done, over, finished. This can be a wonderful relief, like having a great weight lifted off your chest. In essence you've given yourself permission to stop thinking about *him* and start thinking about *you* again. Let's face it, whether you forgive your ex or not isn't going to make any difference to him. He's got other fish to fry. The person you are hurting by hanging on to the hate is yourself.

It is within your power to manifest a good life for yourself. But you need to believe it. And you have to be vigilant. A negative pattern of thinking won't go away overnight. Those traitorous thoughts are going to keep coming back, probably when you least expect them. If you are in a state of abandonment or are worried about money, they are inevitably the kinds of thoughts which will serve you ill:

'I can't cope.'

'The worst things always happen to me.'

'I have no luck.'

But you can nip such thoughts in the bud. The simplest way is this: as soon as they pop into your head, consciously contradict them with a new thought which states the very opposite:

'I am strong enough to cope with anything.'

'The best is yet to come.'

'My luck is changing for the better.'

By stating these things decisively you are halting the 'moan, moan, moan' syndrome and opening yourself up to more positive feedback.

Most people are living back to front. They want to *have* something (a man/loadsamoney) so that they can *do* something (make love/spend, spend, spend) and that will let them *be* something (loved/secure). But what kind of security is it, when someone else can take it away from you without your consent – like your ex has just done? In effect you are allowing another person to have the power over your happiness, to control your life.

The road to real lasting happiness lies the other way round. First you need to *be* something (yourself). Only when you are secure and happy in yourself, in your ability to support yourself emotionally, materially and spiritually, will you have the kind of security that cannot be taken away from you, by anyone, ever. That is when the opportunity to *do* will present itself. A way of life, a job you love. And in doing (the work), you will gain the energy (money) to *have* whatever you want. In *being*, however, you may find that most of the grasping has gone away and you don't really want much at all. You are happy. You are secure. From the inside out.

Security is like a cake. *Doing* is the icing, *having* is the cherry on top. If the icing melts or the dog eats the cherry, they can be replaced. The cake, the centre, the real you, is intact.

Of course you have to find yourself first. Not that this is an easy option. There are so many wrong turnings to lure us off the central path. But the search for self is also the most rewarding and exciting journey you will ever take.

You may need help to cut through the dross, the social conditioning, the things your mother told you (or didn't) and the limitations your lover placed upon you (let me do that, dear, you know you're hopeless with computers). You may have to consult an expert, like a therapist or counsellor. The best will guide rather than lead you through the maze so that the discoveries and the decisions you make are your own rather than the result of someone else's philosophies. Only you know who you really are. Finding out can be fascinating, frustrating and fun.

If you feel you would benefit from professional counselling, ask your doctor to recommend you to someone. Be prepared to wait. When I tried to find a suitable therapist I discovered there was a six-month waiting list. At least it put things in perspective. Up until then I thought I was the only person in the world who had problems. By the time my turn came I'd worked my way through the worst of it myself, so I never did see anyone. If you have the money you might consider going private to be a worthwhile investment. Therapy is no longer a self-indulgent prerogative of the rich. Just remember that there are several different types and you need to find what's right for you.

Whether you take counsel or not, here is a resumé of the positive mental coping strategies described in this book:

- Relaxation, of course.
- Meditation.
- Creative visualization.
- Contemplation – of the good things in your life.
- Affirmations (see Survival Strategy 6).

- Stating the positive.
- Seeking out the self-help section in your local library and devouring anything you can find on the subject. The recommended reading at the back of this book is a starting point. Read a chapter or, if time is pressing, a page every morning or evening to keep the momentum going.
- Avoiding people who moan all the time.
- Trying to see something good in every situation.
- Having a long bath.
- Having a good laugh. (Watch comedies, read a funny book.)
- Cooking something you love.
- Taking a walk.
- Taking a class.
- Taking a deep breath.
- Taking back your power of choice.
- Above all, not being afraid of silence. It's in the eye of silence, when the mind is still, that leaps of intuition and understanding occur.

Recognize the difference between being alone and being lonely. Someone once said that if you're lonely when you're alone, you're in bad company. As your ideas become more upbeat, as you let the negative, limiting thoughts go, as you start to acknowledge your right to happiness, you will find yourself much better company.

Survival Strategy 3
Keep in Touch

For sheer self-indulgence, nothing soothes the spirit or recharges the batteries better than a relaxing, rejuvenating body massage.

It is especially appropriate if your malady is a lack of affection and a shrivelling of the sensuality buds. We touch too little these days and this lack of contact, even between parents and children, turns us in on ourselves so that our troubles, instead of being shared, expand out of all proportion. When we no longer have the option of turning to a partner for comfort, an occasional rubdown can release negative tension from aching muscles before it escalates into permanent pain.

Massage, as with the traditional laying-on of hands, is an ancient therapy which is now gaining ground with a modern medical profession more used to dispensing a pill. Hippocrates recommended it; Julius Caesar and Captain Cook both indulged in it, the former to gain relief from his crippling arthritis, the latter to ease his sciatica. Whereas drugs tend to mask a problem, rather than eliminate it, massage helps the patient recover by lowering the blood-pressure, reducing arousal patterns, allowing the individual to come to terms with their condition or situation and therefore switch to more appropriate forms of behaviour. Symptoms are less likely to recur.

But apart from its benefits in the field of medicine, massage is one of life's unsung luxuries. And in terms of value for money, it is hard to beat. What could be more sybaritic than to lie, cocooned in towels, on a comfortable couch, in a warm room and have aromatic oils rubbed gently into the body? Knots of tension melt under the administrator's practised hands. Circulation picks up, bringing blood and a healthy flush of colour to the skin. The cares of the day are literally stroked away.

Stroking – or effleurage – is one of the basic massage movements. Others include petrissage – a deep, kneading movement, rather like working bread dough – and percussion, where the sides of the hands or fists are used to slap and stimulate the skin.

Massage disciplines can be roughly divided into two camps: East and West; Swedish and shiatsu.

Swedish massage is performed on the naked body using talcum or oils. The Swede Peter Henry Ling revived this ancient art early in the nineteenth century and introduced most of the technical terminology currently in use.

Shiatsu (the Japanese word for a method used in China as early as 3,000 BC) uses acupressure, i.e. pressing with the ball of the thumb and fingers on the same reflex points where acupuncture needles are inserted. The points join to form meridian lines and stimulating them unclogs blockages and allows the *chi* (energy or life-force) to run freely throughout the body. You don't take your clothes off for shiatsu but you are asked to wear something unconstricting and loose such as a track suit.

Reflexology, or foot massage, is a variation of shiatsu. Exponents believe that each part of the body is mirrored by a corresponding point on the foot. If a part of the body is 'out of balance', the relevant area of the foot will feel tender and will respond to massage, which will, in turn, relieve the body's imbalance and restore it to health.

Whatever the theory, it seems that massage relaxes the

body to the extent that the organism's marvellous self-healing powers are allowed to take over.

Most gyms and exercise clubs offer massage, as do alternative health centres and Turkish baths. Don't call any of the numbers you find in the small ads or stuck in telephone boxes. They'll be offering a different kind of service altogether.

One final thought. Practitioners say that giving a massage is as satisfying as taking one. The skill, once learned, can be used on family and friends, children and lovers. It can also be the basis of a business. Training is not exorbitantly expensive or time-consuming, and a spare room can easily be turned into a therapy room. If you are looking for a source of income, it might be worth considering.

7 • Beat the Abandonment Blues

The worst thing about being abandoned is not the sudden drop in income (though that has to run a close second); it's the lack of status and the sudden absence of 'form' in one's life – the *raison d'être*, the thing that gets you out of bed in the morning.

The first casualty is the routine that holds life together. The normal, comforting things that you did as a pair. From early in the morning, when you pour one cup of coffee instead of two, to last thing at night when you have to take on all those little chores that were *his* prerogative – like walking the dog or locking up – life contrives to remind you that there is no longer anyone between you and chaos.

The days stretch ahead – endlessly, hopelessly. Those things you used to do together, like going to the movies or walking on the downs, lose their appeal or become too much trouble, and you can find nothing to replace them. Unless you have the discipline of a job or kids who need taking to school, you find yourself getting up later and later, forgetting to comb your hair, slopping around in your dressing-gown until three in the afternoon.

The less you do, the less you want to do. 'What's the point?' you say. 'Why bother? Who cares?' Before you know it, you are stuck in the slough of despond. You begin to jump when the phone rings, hide behind the curtains when anyone comes to the door. You haven't the will or the energy to go out. You get to the point where, if your Fairy

Beat the Abandonment Blues

Godmother leapt through the window and offered you Prince Charming on a plate, you'd turn him down.

Who could love a slob like you? goes the reasoning. You doubt your ability to cope. You lose all confidence in yourself. You are suffering from negative stress.

Stress is one of the hazards of modern life and it's a blanket word which is much misunderstood. Not all stress is bad for you. Without any we'd fall asleep in a corner and never wake up. There is an optimum stress level at which we function at peak. We are sharp, creative, on top of our form. What most people think of as stress is positive stress, brought on by having too much to do, when we are pushed past our peak into the area of distress. Negative stress, on the other hand, is triggered by having too little to stimulate and excite us. It is suffered by blue-collar workers in repetitive, assembly-line jobs, mothers at home with pre-school children and the newly retired. And whereas an overload of positive stress will lead to such things as hypertension, ulcers, skin disorders and – in extreme cases – heart attacks, an overload of negative stress will almost always lead to depression. And depression, as anyone who has ever suffered that dread affliction knows, is a very difficult cloud to shift once it has settled over your particular horizon.

Here's the scenario. You've lost your man. The world has collapsed around your ears. You want to crawl into bed and never get out again. You feel depleted, drained, debilitated. Nothing interests you. How peaceful it would be to just let go, never ever have to worry about another bill, another problem, another lonely morning. Thoughts of suicide begin to flit into your mind.

How do you halt this dangerous downward spiral?

Believe it or not, one way is to get some exercise.

This may seem like a simplistic solution, but there is sound physiological reasoning behind it. Exercise promotes energy, the kind you desperately need to get you through the crisis. Exercise produces power. The power to carry on. Until things get better.

So if you've been an exerciser before the bombshell dropped, for your welfare's sake don't give it up now. If, on the other hand, you've been using 'family commitments' as an excuse not to work out, then this is the time to start. Regular exercise will arrest the free-fall that leads from the shock of rejection to lack of confidence, serious self-doubt and into the coils of clinical depression.

Regular exercise will give you back your 'get up and go'. It will not only re-energize your body, breathing life into tired limbs and slack muscles, it will make sure that enough oxygen gets pumped into the brain to keep those little grey cells sharp. It will give you the edge you need to start afresh.

Abandoned women are notoriously prone to illness, a lot of it psychologically induced. If there's a virus going round, they'll fall prey to it. The virus makes them feel even more miserable, which leaves them open to even more infection, and so it goes on. The mind is a powerful weapon. People have been known to die from nothing more serious than the lack of the will to live. Exercise can prevent the knock-on effect by stimulating the immune system and raising the spirits.

It will also reintroduce you to the social scene, giving you a place and an opportunity to meet people, to expand your horizons, to get out of the house. It will stop you from becoming alienated from the rest of the human race. Approval is a very solid reinforcer of your own worth when you feel worthless. It's vital at this point to know that other people don't think any less of you just because you've lost the love of one person. If you join a class where nobody knows you, it is especially gratifying to be acknowledged for

Beat the Abandonment Blues

who *you* are, rather than as someone else's shadow.

You will find, too, that most good exercise instructors are excellent motivators, practised in the art of getting the best from everyone and helping everyone get the best from themselves.

Exercise is also one of the most effective beautifiers there is. It not only tones the body, it clears the skin, brightens the eyes and polishes up the hair, all by pumping fresh supplies of good, red, oxygenated blood into the muscles, cells and tissues that make up the basic you. It gives you a glow from within which no amount of expensive cosmetics can achieve (even supposing you could afford them).

And it raises your spirits. This is because it releases endorphins, which are the body's natural opiates, into the bloodstream. If you feel as though you haven't the strength to put one foot in front of the other, don't sit down, it'll only make matters worse. Go for a swim or a walk or, better still, to a movement class. I guarantee you'll have more energy (and hope, enthusiasm and strength) afterwards than you had before.

Exercise is within everyone's budget, no matter how depleted the bank balance. Plump for the best you can afford. It's an investment in your future health and happiness.

If you have enough money to join a fitness club, do so. Not only will you be given a choice of class and machine, but you'll also be able to use lots of stimulating extras like saunas and jacuzzis and in some cases a pool. Fitness clubs are warm and bright and very cheering on a grim, cheerless, post-abandonment day. Some clubs offer massage and beauty therapy (remember this when Christmas comes around and your mother or girlfriend or daughter asks you what present you want).

If a club in the private sector is out of your financial reach, check out the local council facilities. These are often better equipped than the 'posher' places and cost a fraction of the price.

If even that's beyond your means, look in your local paper or newsagent's windows for independent classes run on a pay-as-you-come basis. Compare the cost of a class with the price of a hair-do or facial. Although the latter are enjoyable and luxurious, they are 'surface' treatments, effective for a very short time. Exercise will get right down to the core of things, to the centre of your being. Done regularly, its benefits will last you a lifetime.

If you're totally broke and think you can't afford anything at all, running, or (if you're more mature or *really* out of condition) walking, costs nothing at all. As does swimming, if you happen to be lucky enough to live by the sea.

Exercise is not only great for the body, it's wonderful for rekindling a sense of self. One of the joys of being a fitness professional is to see people come into a class for the first time looking grey and unfit and uneasy, and then watch them blossom and grow and change. Within weeks they will be shucking off their baggy tracksuits and appearing in bright leotards. As their bodies firm and their faces brighten they start to make other, more cosmetic changes. Mousy hair takes on warm coppery tones or even turns spectacularly blonde, newfound cheekbones get a little more emphasis with blusher, body lotions appear in sports bags for application after the shower. People rediscover themselves, regain their sense of identity or, better still, invent a new, more exciting persona. Some clients change out of all recognition; all of them change, and invariably for the better.

Nor does age exclude you from this marvellous elixir of life. Current research shows that you can improve muscle tone, cardiac fitness and flexibility well into your seventies. Even after that, exercise can stop things deteriorating. And it is great insurance against osteoporosis, the bone-softening disease which afflicts so many women after menopause and which, unchecked, can lead to such unsightly conditions as dowager's hump.

Movement is life – whether you're fifteen or fifty. So keep moving.

There is nothing quite as exhilarating as the adrenalin rush brought on by a good work-out. It's like champagne without the hangover. It will make you feel better about yourself, about your prospects.

If you take a morning class (before work or straight after you've dropped the kids at school) it will give you the energy to bounce through the rest of the day. If you have neither offspring nor work, it will give your life shape and focus, something to get out of bed for. If you take an evening class (or run, swim, whatever), it will stop you spending every night slumped in front of the telly and make sure that your social life doesn't grind to a complete standstill. (For more on exercise see Survival Strategy 4, Fit For Life.)

Exercise is a positive thing. And positive action leads to positive thinking. Being abandoned is demoralizing in the extreme. Exercise will keep up your morale.

So take your trainers in one hand and your courage in the other and get started.

Other ways to get a grip:

- Don't go to pot – **go on retreat**. If you crave peace and quiet and don't mind Spartan surroundings, a break at a monastery or a nunnery could work wonders. If you're in Scotland, the Findhorn Foundation do retreat weeks as does the Buddhist enclave on Holy Island. You don't have to be a believer to take advantage of some cloistered calm. Contact the National Retreat Centre (see Useful Addresses) for information on where to start.

- If you feel you can't unburden yourself to family or friends, **try counselling**. A friendly, unbiased, professional stranger can often be a better sounding-board than a bosom buddy who (with the best of intentions) re-inforces your negative outlook by bad-mouthing your ex rather than forcing you to face your own accountability.

- **See your doctor**. She or he won't have time to listen to your tale of woe but will be able to recommend you to a counsellor and/or give you a *short-term* prescription for tranquillizers or sleeping pills to help you over the worst.

- **Alternative therapies** can be wonderful stress relievers and a little hands-on work (massage, reflexology, shiatsu, acupuncture) can make you feel pampered and cherished when you need it most.

After a suitable grieving period you owe it to yourself to make a positive effort to recover mentally and physically. All of us have inner reserves which are greater than we realize. Self-image and self-worth are important elements on the road to recovery. Respect yourself or no one else will. Choose enabling coping strategies that will help you through the pain rather than deadening it:

- **Lay off pills, booze, chocolates.**
- **Sleep a lot.**
- **Take warm baths.** If you can't afford bubbles, use washing-up liquid – saves cleaning the bath. Soften the skin with supermarket baby lotion.
- Have a **facial**, get a new **hair cut** or indulge in a **massage** on the cheap (maybe even free) – local hairdressing/beauty schools are always looking for clients on whom students can practise. They are supervised by expert instructors so, don't worry, you won't come out

looking like Ken Dodd. They also do manicures, pedicures, eyebrow-plucking, leg-waxing and G5 (massage with a machine) – all the things you'd expect to find in a 'proper' salon.

- **Update your image.** Scour women's magazines for ideas for a new you. If you're unhappy with how you look, change it. Is it *your* image – or was it his? If you're happy in principle, aim for a slimmer, sleeker, more sensational version.

- **Eat for energy not comfort** (see Survival Strategy 9).

- If you have £1.00 left over at the end of the week, spend it on a **lottery ticket**. It could be you. If you win, have a face-lift or a fortnight at Champneys or a trip to Armani. If you feel like Methuselah's mother, book a holiday to the Valley of the Kings. It's reassuring to know that *something*'s older than you.

8 • Massaging the Ego

Twelve ways to build up self-esteem:

1. Take an assertiveness course.
If you've always been a browbeaten mouse, an assertiveness course will give you the courage of your convictions. If, on the other hand, you lose your rag and become aggressive whenever anyone questions your judgement (a sure sign of stress), it will teach you to speak up without alienating the opposition. It's all about stating your needs clearly and concisely. (Easier said than done if you are being patronized by your ex's lawyer or dismissed as a featherhead by a prospective employer.) It's also about win/win situations, negotiating and ultimately getting what you want. Assertiveness is a handy strategy in many areas, from returning shoddy goods to dealing with officious civil servants. One of the more useful hints is not to get into an argument but instead to repeat your request over and over in a calm, clear voice: 'I'd like my money back, please'. Much more effective than having an attack of the screaming meemies in the middle of the shop.

More and more councils and education authorities are running assertiveness courses (many aimed at women returners) and there are numerous books on the subject. Check the adult education department of your local college or your nearest library for details.

2. Ask yourself motivating questions.
Start each day by asking yourself questions like:

'What good things are going to happen today?'

'What do I hope to achieve from this meeting?'

'How can I use my time most effectively?'

Questions like these will focus the mind and create an expectation of success, whereas . . .

'What can go wrong today?'

'Why am I bothering to go to this meeting when no one's going to listen to me?'

'How am I going to get through all this without having a nervous breakdown?'

. . . will set you up for failure before you even start.

Both sets of questions apply to the same set of circumstances. The only thing that's different is the perspective.

3. Buy or borrow personal development books or tapes.
Read a chapter every day, preferably in the morning, and use the information until it becomes second nature. A positive approach to life is like a strong body: it needs regular exercise. If time is precious, listen to tapes in what the Americans call 'windscreen time' – while driving to work or, if you travel by public transport, during your journey. If you have small children, settle down with a mug of cocoa and read your chapter when they've gone to bed.

4. Buy a mug with 'I love you' on it.

5. Remind yourself constantly of your good points.
We Brits are a nation of self-deprecators. We are brought up to think it's 'not quite nice' to blow our own trumpet. Having a good opinion of yourself is nothing to do with being bumptious or 'showing off'. And it's certainly a more

effective way to live life than constantly putting yourself down. This doesn't mean you should turn a blind eye or condone bad or tricksy behaviour in yourself. If you have less than admirable aspects to your character (and don't we all?), acknowledge them and resolve to improve. Be vigilant about negative thinking and try to stop it once and for all.

6. Review your lists often.
See Chapters 3, 4 and 5.

7. Try to learn a new skill every year (whatever your age).
Word-processing. Swimming. Car maintenance. You cannot have enough life skills. Your new knowledge needn't make you money, just as long as it enriches your experience. If you are a career girl, add to your qualifications, don't just rest on your laurels. Go to conferences, seminars, workshops on your subject. Keep up to date. If you want to break through the glass ceiling, you need to compete as an equal.

8. Watch your vocabulary.
Don't say your boyfriend, husband or significant other has run away and left you. Say you're 'between relationships'. This smacks of choice rather than necessity. To you as well as everyone else. Similarly, if someone asks what you do, don't say you're 'just a housewife'. Apart from being bloody hard work, being a home-maker is one of the most worthwhile, honourable and complicated professions there is. The reason it's held in such low esteem is because it's so badly paid. Think how much it would cost to pay professionals to do all the jobs it can cover: cook, child-minder, educator, house-keeper, laundrymaid, valet, gardener. And most of us do it for room and board!

9. Remember that there is a difference between a healthy ego and vanity.

If you succeed at something, don't be afraid to tell everybody. And congratulate yourself. Mark each milestone with a reward, even if it's only a pat on the back.

10. Keep a journal and record even your smallest victories and triumphs.

If you make a mistake, focus on what you learned from that and resolve not to do it again. Then *forget it* and move on. Day to day these life events may not seem to amount to much but this time next year, when you review them, you will have a clear record of just how far you've progressed as a human being.

11. If you have children, think of them.

Encourage a healthy self-esteem in your children by praising them often. Children, like plants, flourish in an atmosphere of approval. Give them the confidence to be the best they can be without pressurizing them to be the best in the class.

Don't try to live through them or expect them to fulfil the fantasies you never managed to attain. Don't choose a profession for them ('My son's going to be a doctor'). Allow them to follow their own heart. Better they should be a happy window-cleaner than a miserable lawyer.

Naturally you need house rules. Make sure they understand them. And stick to them. You don't want to live with a bunch of savages. Remember that bad behaviour is always the fault of the parent, not the child. And nobody likes a spoiled brat. So be firm but fair. Children are much more secure when they know how far they can go. And they generally respond favourably to an expectation of good behaviour.

Never threaten anything you don't intend to carry out – 'If you do that again, I'll smack you.' If they do it and you don't, you've undermined your authority for all time. Conversely, try not to say 'no' just for the sake of it.

Set an example. Don't expect them to conform to rules you're not prepared to stick to yourself, such as 'Stop shouting!'

Don't whinge, or nag, or moan, or blackmail, or manipulate. Never say, 'After all I've done for you,' or, 'Because I say so!'

Avoid embarrassing them in public – don't wear your mini-skirt to the prize-giving, flirt with their boyfriends, simper 'everyone takes us for sisters', get drunk anywhere their best friend's mother is going to see you.

You don't own your children. They are the future. You are lucky enough to be able to borrow them for a while. Make the most of it. Before you know it, they'll be grown up with children of their own.

Your reward will be when they come to visit because they want to, because they like you, trust you, love you. Not because you expect it, or because you'll make them feel guilty if they don't, or because it's their duty.

Your kids don't owe you anything. You owe them all the love you've got to give. And then some. Watching them turn into independent human beings is one of the best boosts to your own self-image that you could ever hope to have.

12. Being judgemental is always a cheap shot.

Feeling smug about others' shortcomings is not the way to boost your own self-esteem. You don't make your reputation by denigrating other people – unless you're aiming for a reputation as a critical harpy. People are doing the best they can under the circumstances in which they find themselves or according to the life lessons they've learned so far. Mr Jones' drinking or Mrs Smith's décolletage really are none of your concern.

Massaging the Ego

Criticism of others comes from severe *lack* of self-esteem. It's an unendearing way to make yourself feel superior at another person's expense. To paraphrase the Bible, it's better to worry about the beam in your own eye than point out the mote in somebody else's.

And if people judge you? Well, again, that's their problem. You know who you are. If you're doing the best you can, that's all anyone can ask of you. Or you can ask of yourself.

Survival Strategy 4
Fit For Life

Making your mind up to start an exercise regime is one thing, but more difficult by far and infinitely more important is the decision to keep it up – to get out of that warm bed on a rainy Saturday morning and go to class; to don your track suit after a hard day's work when all you really want to do is head for the nearest armchair and sit down.

Exercise is for life, *your* life, whatever the weather, whatever the temptations not to do it. You must keep it up if you want to get, and stay, fit. The good thing is, it gets easier as you go along. That's because once you've got yourself into shape, your energy starts to soar, your sleep-pattern improves, your skin starts to glow and your brain feels sharp as a tack regardless of being under pressure; persistent colds dry up and breathlessness becomes a thing of the past.

If your get-up-and-go has got-up-and-gone, then regular exercise will make you feel really alive for the first time since you were a kid and spent your days running and climbing and skipping.

Irregular exercise is a waste of time. Worse – it can be dangerous.

Those who exercise in fits and starts tend to fling themselves into activity with the desperation born of knowing that they have let things slide too far. They want to do something about it *right away*. The result? Stiffness in the muscles. Soreness in the joints. Disillusion in the soul.

Two things to remember about exercise:

1. It should be regular.
2. You shouldn't outpace yourself.

First decide what you're going to do. Pick something you like. It is immaterial initially whether you go to an aerobics class or play squash or swim. Then decide how many times a week you are going to do it. Don't be over-ambitious at this point.

Keep in mind that when you are building an exercise routine into your life-style you'll need to include not just the hour when you're actually working out, but the length of time it takes to get to and from the pool, club or studio, plus twenty minutes to change, shower and, if need be, dry your hair.

Next, check out the facilities in your area. Try them out, one by one. Most clubs will give you a trial run. If not, forget it – there's got to be a catch. Go for the cleanest, closest, friendliest place with the brightest instructors (not necessarily in that order). Never settle for anything that's just OK. Unless you look forward to going, you won't go.

Work out at least twice a week. *Every week.*

Three times a week (or every other day) is the ideal. That's because, in theory, strenuous exercise raises the metabolic rate and keeps it raised for a significant number of hours after you stop. Also because the muscles, which sustain small tears during the work-out, need time to rest and recuperate. But if you are just starting, three times a week can be a high ideal to live up to, especially if you have a demanding job, an active social life or a family to cope with.

Better to exercise twice a week, regularly, to begin with, than set your sights too high, miss a few sessions, become disenchanted and give up the whole thing. You'll be back to square one and you will have wasted all that valuable effort. It's the same with dieting.

Say you've been extra good for three weeks, two days and fifteen minutes and then you fall off the wagon and succumb to a chocolate biscuit. What do you do? Say, 'Naughty, naughty', and decide not to do it again? No. You figure, 'Oh, well, since I've cheated anyway . . .' You devour the whole packet. In half an hour you replace the five pounds you so painstakingly lost.

Not that you should be dieting at all. Dieting is so negative. It should be re-titled denyeting, since you're constantly having to deny yourself: I mustn't (eat cookies); I shouldn't (have an extra helping).

What you should be doing is thinking positively about what you're putting into your body. A healthy diet rather than on/off dieting is the secret to staying slim.

And, if you need to or want to lose weight, the way to go about it is by raising your metabolic rate so that your body burns up calories faster, thus replacing wobbly fat with streamlined muscle.

You can raise your metabolic rate permanently by taking regular exercise. You won't raise anything by working out once a month. Except maybe a laugh when you struggle into your shorts.

Bodies are like cars. If you service them regularly, feed them the right fuel and treat them with a little tender loving care, they will serve you well and last a long time. If you don't, they will break down.

The only difference is – you can replace your car.

9 • Home Sweet Home
or How to Make Your House Pay for Itself

There is no Fairy Godmother. It's 'do it yourself' time. The sooner you realize that, and accept it, the happier you will be.

With acceptance comes responsibility – a scary concept, but also a liberating one. For taking responsibility is a learnable skill, and it gives us a sense of power and self-worth that is truly amazing.

There is a theory which states that in life we are all where we deserve to be. Through the decisions that we made, or didn't make, the challenges we shirked, the blind eyes we turned, we are where we are because of our own past behaviour. Cause and effect. This may sound harsh, unjust, uncompromising or just plain unacceptable – 'Now you're telling me it's *my* fault!' – but in a strange way it can also be a very comforting concept. If we are in the soup as a result of our own choices, then at least we are not the victims of some malevolent fate. This itself puts us back in control. All we need to do to make a better future is to make better choices.

Easier said than done. Knowledge is the first step, but knowing isn't doing. In a sense we are programmed to behave in certain ways. But being aware of these patterns at least allows us the *possibility* of change. We need no longer be victims of our own ignorance.

So, if you're one of those women who has always

relegated the paying of bills to your other half, now's the time to get your act together.

The first, and most important priority must be to secure the roof over your head.

A place of one's own represents stability; if it is threatened by your ex's exit, what do you do?

If you and your partner have been renting, you can just give notice and go. Another roof, town, country, continent. What's stopping you? Provided you aren't locked into a career structure or a negative-equity situation, you are free to do whatever you want, go wherever you like. Whoopee! Even if you had your whole life strategy planned out, you might consider a sabbatical. There is nothing like a change of scene to get things into perspective and heal a broken heart.

Otherwise, unless the memories are horrendous, *don't* sell up or move out. Stay put. Especially if money is tight or you have children to consider or both. Moving house can be unbelievably expensive, and in leaving the district you will lose friends, familiarity of routine, and support systems which may have taken years to build up. Extra upheaval will add not only to your stress levels but to those of any children involved. Coming to terms with their father's defection will be destabilizing enough without the extra trauma of losing their friends and having to move to a new school.

Even considering the downturn in the market, property is a valuable asset. Not just as an investment, but also in terms of your credit rating. It is much easier to raise a loan to launch a business or buy a new car if you have a house or a flat as collateral.

So if you've got property, try to hold on to it, at least until the dust settles.

Make an appointment with the manager of the building society or bank which holds your mortgage and lay your situation on the line. Contrary to common supposition, mortgage lenders don't want to repossess. It's not in their interest. They may well be willing to cut your payments until you get back on your feet. In my case they helped get the house transferred to my name. Initially they wouldn't accept me as mortgagee because of my erratic earning potential but the manager and my accountant worked out a deal whereby the endowment policy held by myself and my ex was cashed in to reduce the debt. My half brought the loan down to an amount where they were willing to take a chance on me. They even let me keep £1,500 of the lump sum to pay for badly needed repairs to the roof. The rest I raised from a local government grant. There is always a way round things if you're prepared to be up-front and negotiate. It's when you ignore threatening letters, allow debts to accumulate and pretend that it isn't happening that the roof caves in. Don't on any account let your ex bully you into selling. If the mortgage is in joint names, as long as you continue to meet the payments, he can't get you out. When you decide to sell, you'll have to give him half the profit, but until then try to maintain your standard of living by staying where you are. Selling up and moving down merely means less value for your money.

If you're not working you may not know how you're going to keep up the payments. In certain circumstances the DSS will help with mortgages or cover rent. Your next move should be to see them and find out exactly what you're entitled to in the way of help. The rules are constantly changing and can be complicated so your best bet is to approach them directly and as soon as possible.

If, like I did, you don't qualify for government assistance yet the jobs available don't pay enough to cover the outgoings, don't despair. There are other ways to avoid the nightmare of homelessness.

If you have a spare bedroom or two, one of the most obvious is to take in a lodger.

Rules and Regulations

Should you decide on this as a strategy, you will need to make some adjustments. None of them will be as uncomfortable as being thrown out on the street. I had to get used to getting dressed first thing instead of writing in my dressing-gown until noon.

You will also have to make some rules. Mine were no smoking and no bonking. With a fourteen-year-old in the house I didn't want to suddenly turn the place into a den of iniquity. Speaking of which, if you are young and desirable, it might be sensible to stick to female guests. It's not professional to 'get involved', and the neighbours will talk. Plus, if you are on any form of social security, the DSS may reach their own conclusions (erroneous or not) and cut your benefit.

Options

Before you drum up some custom you will need to decide whether you are offering room only (much less bother) or providing breakfast and/or an evening meal (means you can charge more and if you're at home and cooking anyway . . .). Are you letting the room on a permanent basis, weekly, or daily (as in bed and breakfast)? Each has its pros and cons.

If you take a permanent lodger, you will be able to ask for your rent monthly in advance. You will also be able to ask for a month's rent as a deposit. Be sure you do. Then if your tenant does a moonlight, you'll have time to fill the vacancy without being out of pocket. The deposit will also cover breakages but not normal wear and tear. NB: *never* spend the deposit. You need to have it available to give back when your lodger moves on. Keep it in a deposit account where it'll give a little interest. Permanent lodgers should give a month's notice or forfeit the deposit. Similarly, you'll need to give them the same amount of time to find a new place if things aren't working out. Fair's fair. Put the arrangement in writing, including house rules, whether or not you provide washing facilities or do their laundry, what happens about the phone-bill, if they're expected to be up at a certain time on a certain day so that the cleaning lady can change the sheets – all those little items that can lead to friction. If they are written down, there's no margin for misunderstanding.

If you live in (or outside) a city where there's a particular industry (in Aberdeen it was oil), you may get people who work on contract but who have homes and families to which they return at the weekend. Commercial travellers also fall into this category. It's not worth their while to have a flat. They may be working all the hours God sends and, when they come back from the office, factory or rig, they want to know their bed's made and (if you're providing food) that there's a meal on the table. A home from home, in fact. They are also glad to have some company of an evening rather than having to hang around in pubs. The advantage of weekly paying guests is that they pay a slightly higher rate than a permanent lodger. Also, you'll have your weekends free.

Bed and breakfast brings in the highest return – in theory. You can charge by the day and let the room as a single or a double. In practice, you may be empty more days than not, so it evens out. When you do have customers, you have to change the beds daily rather than weekly, which means extra hassle and laundry bills. There's also the expense of advertising, although after you've been up and running for a while you will start to get return bookings, provided you're offering the kind of accommodation and service that warrants it.

You may have to try all three options before you find the one that suits you. After a few false starts I came down to this: I offered one room with use of the kitchen (for cooking and laundry). Lodgers could then come in and cook whenever it was convenient for them and sleep as late as they liked at weekends. I didn't charge extra for utilities, but I had the phone-bill itemized so that we could work out who owed what.

I had one permanent lodger to ensure that basic bills were met and I occasionally took in people from the local theatre to cover extras, treats or unexpected bills. Theatre work is erratic but fun. The stars obviously stay at big hotels (so don't expect Tom Conti to suddenly arrive on the doorstep) but if there's a show with a big cast there are a lot of people looking for digs. Theatre people are no trouble. They sleep late so they're never in the bathroom or the kitchen when anyone else wants to be, they eat breakfast mid-morning and have their baths mid-afternoon. They're out in the evening so they're not hanging around the lounge watching the TV when you want to put your feet up and relax. And as a bonus they can sometimes get you complimentary tickets to the show – a real treat if you're on a strict budget and can't afford such luxuries. Some people are wary of theatre folk. They think they're going to come in drunk at all hours and wreck the place (that's rock bands). But having spent many years 'on tour' when I was a singer, I know that decent digs are a godsend to the itinerant performer and, far from abusing your hospitality, when they find somewhere warm and comfortable to stay 'strolling players' will respect your house as they would their own and come back to stay every time they pass through town. I had a couple of boys from the Scottish ballet who wouldn't go anywhere else. They used to book three months in advance to make sure they got to stay with me.

How to Find Clients

Call the local theatre and ask to go on their digs' list. They will advise you of the going rates. Stick an ad on the notice-board back-stage for good measure. Plug any particular selling features, such as 'Quiet house' (means they can sleep late in peace), 'Within walking distance of the theatre' (means they don't have to fork out for late-night taxis).

If you want a permanent resident, you could do worse than start with a student. Get out your *Yellow Pages* and look up all the local colleges, training centres and universities. They are always desperate for space. Call the accommodation department. They will put your details on their database and your particulars on the student notice-board. Student lets are seasonal. You're more likely to get a placement in late August than mid-October. However, it's worth passing on your details at any time: students may hate where they're staying and want to move half-way through a term. The down-side is that most students generally go home for the holidays and, subsisting as they do on grants, haven't the wherewithal to pay for the room in their absence. So you could have large gaps of a month at a time in your financial year. On the other hand, if you have an offspring at university who wants to come home in the holidays, the arrangement could work out very well. Otherwise, if you want a year's unbroken contract, try for a foreign student, who won't be able to afford to go home for every vacation, or, better still, a young visiting foreign-exchange lecturer, who has the advantage of being on salary. A word of warning: because grants are so low nowadays it's best to get your whole term's rent up-front. There are students who, faced with a largish cheque, visit every watering hole in town in the first week of term and find themselves financially embarrassed a month before the holidays. You are doing yourself (and their liver) a favour by ensuring that they don't spend the rent money on Murphy's.

If you live in a big town, contact the BBC and the independent TV and radio stations. They often have visiting producers on short-term contracts and technical staff on temporary placement.

Get in touch with the personnel department of national companies such as Marks and Spencer or large industries which may recruit from around the country. Often executives will spend up to six months in digs while looking for a permanent home into which to move the family. If they can't sell their house back home, what began as a temporary arrangement may become a permanent one. Some companies work with 'placement services' who specialize in re-locating families. They also often want temporary accommodation for commuting executives, so it's worth letting them know what you've got available.

If you've decided to offer bed and breakfast, get in touch with your local tourist board. They will send someone round to view the property and tell you whether it's up to their standards. If it is, they'll give you a quality rating (two crossed fig leaves on a J-cloth or whatever) and put you on their books. For a yearly fee they will advertise your facilities in their literature and send along customers. You have to conform to certain rules and pay a percentage for any business they put your way, but it's a good way to get started.

Whichever option you choose, don't advertise in the local paper unless you absolutely have to – it is prohibitively expensive, and as you have to give out your phone number, anyone, including Jack the Ripper, might ring up. At least working through companies or universities you have some kind of safeguard. As a woman on your own you can't be too careful.

If you do decide to advertise, be specific. For example,

'Young professional woman, non-smoker, wanted to share room in family home'. Then if someone unsuitable calls, you have an excuse. Don't feel obliged to give your address over the phone and if you don't like the sound of the person, you can always say the room's gone. My advice would be to buy the paper and look in the accommodation-wanted ads. That way you hold all the aces. You can ring *them* up. If they're not kosher, they don't have your number and you're only out the cost of a paper and a phone-call. If you *really* want to keep the costs down, your local library will carry the daily newspapers plus any local trade journals which may also carry accommodation-wanted ads.

The legal implications for taking in lodgers are minimal. You can take five people without registering as a guesthouse or applying for change of use. Under the 'rent a room' scheme you are allowed to make up to £55 a week without paying tax. You'll need to adjust your house insurance and inform your mortgage company. In theory building societies disapprove of lodgers; in practice, provided you're discreet about it, they usually turn a blind eye. As I said before, they'd much rather have the mortgage paid than have to repossess. But do check.

Other Ways to Make Income from Your Home

1. If you have a garage that you no longer need (because you've sold your car or because your ex has taken the one you shared), you can let that. Charge according to the area. The 'garages wanted' small ads in the paper will give ball-park figures. Clearly city-centre lets attract higher rents than those in the suburbs. However, with car insurance rocketing, even garages further out are well worth letting – the lessee can often make the rent back in saved premiums. And you've realized a little income for spare space. One point:

make sure the person you are letting to wants the space to park his or her car. Some are looking for premises to run 'homers', i.e. small black-market businesses doing car repairs or carpentry. They may even want the 'lock-up' to store bent goods à la Arthur Daley. Don't get involved. If anything goes wrong, your insurance won't cover it. And ignorance is no defence in the eyes of the law.

To find clients, again look in the local press. Or place an ad in your local newsagent's window. I went to every office in the adjacent street, said I had a garage space to let and left my card. I had five offers by the end of the afternoon. If you get a proper contract, with payment twelve weeks in advance, keep the contract on file and mark the payment dates in your diary so you can send reminder invoices.

Parking space is at such a premium in big towns that, even if you don't have a garage, you might be able to rent forecourt space. At a tenner a week it's still cheaper than parking meters. I even know someone who rented their resident's parking space after they sold their car.

Try not to let garage space to a lodger, even if you can charge extra for it. If they leave, you will have lost two sources of revenue in one hit. Hedge your bets.

2. If you can't afford a holiday but desperately want a break, you could exchange with someone elsewhere in the world or let the house for a fortnight and take a vacation on the proceeds. There are specialist companies that deal with this kind of exchange. For a minimal yearly fee they will advertise your house in a quarterly property mailing. Prospective exchangers then get in touch with you or you with them. For about £25.00 and the fares, you could be spending the summer in Miami. Two such companies are listed under Useful Addresses; a browse through the small ads of any travel magazine will turn up several others.

3. If you really can't cover the mortgage, an alternative to selling is to let the entire house. This should not only pay the outgoings but give you enough income to live elsewhere. Again, the universities will consider taking over a whole house (on a yearly contract basis) as will relocation agencies and some estate agencies (although the latter will charge about 10 per cent as a placement fee). Some agencies specialize in foreign clients. Different nationalities look for different things in a let. Japanese businessmen will pay high rents but are very discerning, so your property needs to be pretty plush. The French want character and a nice kitchen. The Americans aren't interested unless you have two bathrooms, air conditioning, a dishwasher and a forty-foot lounge. The DSS is also looking for accommodation for families and people on the dole.

Suppose you want to let the whole place for a short period only. If you live in Edinburgh you can get premium rates for your garden shed during the Festival, so check with your local tourist office whether your area has a similar shindig coming up. And a four-week let during the panto season can bring in enough to pay the mortgage for three months. Stay with relatives if you have them. Otherwise use a little lateral thinking: let the house, cover the month's outgoings and use the excess to have four weeks in the Bahamas!

The Bottom Line

Given the worst possible scenario – no work and foreclosure by the building society – all is still not lost. You could solve both problems by taking a position with 'live-in' accommodation. Depending on your age and qualifications (or lack of them), you could try for a job as a housekeeper, companion, nanny, au pair, secretary, barmaid, school matron or minder at a local authority children's home. If you are willing to move from place to place, a company called Country Cousins (see Useful Addresses) specializes in providing short-term companions to look after elderly people in their own homes. They pay about £150.00 a week but it's all found. They particularly like more mature people with nurturing skills and a sense of responsibility.

To Sum Up

If you have a small flat, you could share a bedroom as a stop-gap. If you have a house with three or four unused bedrooms you could make a tidy business out of your family home. I enjoyed the experience of having a houseful of people so much I would have been happy to have done just that if I'd had the space. Unfortunately, I only had one free bedroom so the scheme was never going to do more than cover the outgoings.

So how, if I only had one extra bedroom, could I have a permanent lodger and still squeeze in the occasional theatrical? Simple. When His Majesty's called I gave up my own room and slept on a mattress in the study. The door was always closed so nobody knew and the extras paid not only the utilities but left enough over for the odd bottle of Rioja.

If the idea appals you, remember – it was my choice. Nobody was making me do it. It was a very comfortable mattress, sleeping on the floor did wonders for my back, and the extra money gave me the freedom to stay in the security of my own home until I was ready to move on to bigger and better things.

10 • Financial Fitness: Part I

Catch-22

A man is not a meal-ticket. If you are a free spirit with no dependants, then after communal property has been split, you have no more right to expect him to keep you in the manner to which you have become accustomed when he moves on than he would if the situation were reversed. Like it or not, as a grown-up person you should be responsible for yourself.

But what if you are *not* a free spirit? What if there are children in the equation?

In theory no man should be able to desert his family and get away scot-free. In practice it happens all the time. Many men, quite simply, up sticks and disappear. Many more carry on living under the noses of their desertees while using every loophole in the law to avoid their obligations.

If he is in work, you have some hope of recompense – maintenance payments can be stopped at source and paid directly to the mother. But if he's self-employed, it's another story entirely. If he does not submit proper accounts for his tax returns there is no way of proving how much he's making; he can plead poverty till the cows come home. If you're lucky enough to get legal aid, you can take him to court, but there is no way you can actually *make* him pay up. Of course you can have him put in gaol, eventually, for non-payment. But what good will that do you? All you've done is waste precious time and energy, and you still have nothing to show for it except your nineteenth nervous breakdown.

So how do you nab the blackguard?

My advice is, don't even bother to try. Put your energy to more productive use. If you inject half the effort that you would expend pursuing court orders and filling in forms into more positive pursuits, such as generating some income of your own, you'll feel twice as happy and only a quarter as helpless.

I know it's not fair that he should get away with it. But then, who ever said life was fair?'

If, despite the fact that it will leave you bitter and twisted, you still want to screw him for every penny he's got, contact your nearest Citizens Advice Bureau. They will be able to tell you whether or not you qualify for legal aid. You should find their number in the front of your local Thomson's Directory.

Don't, on any account, use your own money to pay for a lawyer. We are talking bottomless pits here.

And the best of British luck!!

Ways to Generate Money

1. Contact the **Child Support Agency** and let them do the dirty work for you. If they get you some money, well and good, but don't hold your breath. Unless your ex is in gainful employment and you know his whereabouts, they may not be terribly useful. They will put out a trace on your nearest (if not dearest), but if you're not already on Supplementary Benefit, let me warn you up front that there is a charge for this service It was £40.00 when I enquired, with no guarantee they would find the wandering boy, and the amount of my entitlement, should they succeed, set at the princely

sum of £2.50 a week. Quite frankly for me it wasn't worth the hassle, but it's worth a phone-call to find out where you stand.

2. Go to the **Department of Social Security** and check out your benefit situation.

The frustrating way to do this is to go along unannounced, sit in various queues for hours on end, fill in innumerable, almost incomprehensible forms, many of which will demand information which you won't have available, and get thoroughly brought down. If you are also accompanied by small, easily bored children, the mind boggles.

The efficient way to do it is to call first, explain your situation briefly, make an appointment and ask them to send you the relevant forms. You will be astounded at the amount of bumf that arrives. However, at least you will be able to fill in the paperwork in your own time, in your own home, with the necessary information to hand. Then you can take the completed forms with you to your interview. If it's humanly possible, leave the kid/s with someone else. Be prepared to wait, even with an appointment, and to feel depressed. Social Security offices are very depressing places. That's why it's a good idea not to frequent them more often, or for longer, than is absolutely necessary.

The benefits system is complicated and not userfriendly, especially if you are in a state of emotional disrepair. The rules are complex and constantly changing, as are the amounts involved. But if you're at home with small children and not working, you should be entitled to Income Support and to have your rent or mortgage and rates paid. Even if you're doing a part-time, lowpaid, second-income job, your pay packet should be topped up by Family Credit to what the government considers to be subsistence level. But there's the rub. It will only *ever* be subsistence level. And you and yours deserve a better future than that. So try to look on any kind of benefit as a stopgap until you've got your act together. Not that you shouldn't claim any entitlement, but state hand-outs do have a way of sapping the entrepreneurial strength and trapping you in dependant mode.

You may find, as I did, that you fall into a poverty trap where the money offered wouldn't even cover the bills on the house, let alone food, petrol and clothing (not exactly luxury items). When I pointed this out, I was told by an extremely patronizing clerk that I would need to budget. It doesn't matter how well you budget, if your outgoings are more than your income, you're never going to balance the books. So for me all the form-filling went for naught. It was back to the drawing-board.

3. **One Parent Benefit**. Whoever it was that passed the legislation to put Family Allowance in the mother's name should be canonized forthwith. Get a form from your Post Office straight away and apply for the extra One Parent Benefit to which you are now entitled. This is extremely straightforward. Everyone qualifies regardless of income and you can usually backdate payments to when your man ran out on you.

4. Some men don't evade their financial responsibilities entirely. They play a power game where they use money to keep you in a constant state of insecurity. They do pay, sometimes . . . but so erratically that you don't know from one week to the next whether you are solvent or not. If this is happening and you know where

he works, for speed and efficiency and to stop the inevitable cycle of begging or screaming down the phone, go directly to his boss. Take the children with you. No need to behave badly (you don't want him to earn sympathy); simply put the matter straight. Some companies will look favourably on an application to have maintenance deducted direct from the father's pay packet. A phone-call to your man threatening this action may be enough to get him to cough up to avoid embarrassment.

5. Contact his **trade union** if he belongs to one. Even if you don't know where he is, they might. Also, most trade unions are very family orientated and have contingency hardship funds for precisely the situation you now find yourself in. If you don't ask, you won't get.

6. If you have ever worked and were, or still are, a trade union member, apply to the union on your own behalf. As a thirty-year member of British Actors Equity Association, I did so when an expected lodger let me down at the last minute and I was literally on my uppers. Even though I'd been virtually 'resting' for ten years and therefore paying the lowest rates, the union contacted the benevolent fund, who sent a cheque for £350 in the next post. The money made sure we didn't starve over Christmas. It also did something to rekindle a faith in humanity which a succession of government agencies had almost succeeded in extinguishing. I intend to use some of the proceeds of this book to reimburse the fund. As they say, 'Don't repay a kindness – pass it on.' The union also waived my membership for the year. So if membership fees themselves are a consideration, it might be worth asking your union to 'lodge your card' until you are back on your feet.

7. Ask a **charity**. Don't be proud. That's what they're there for. We tend to think of a charity as being something to which we give money. Consider all the donations you've made in the past. If you're in genuine need, now's the time to claim some back. Many charities are sitting on unclaimed money simply because people don't know it's there. Some may give a lump sum for a specific item like school shoes. Others may even gift a weekly stipend to tide you over the worst.

   Look in your library for a list of local and national charities. Pick out the ones that are relevant to your situation. Not all will apply. Some have qualifying clauses and most are quite specific in their area of gifting. All will need proof of your income (or lack of it) and outgoings. Clearly, they need to make sure you're a genuine case and not some unscrupulous chancer trying to make a quick buck. But most charities are sensitive and unobtrusive. We've come a long way since the days of *Oliver Twist*. When you've sorted out some likely prospects, call and ask for an application form, fill it in and keep your fingers crossed.

8. Ask the **family**. If you have a close relative whom you know has made provision for you in their will, ask if you can have the money now, when you need it.

Ways to Cut Out Unnecessary Expenditure

1. If you are a working woman, go through your file and cancel any annual membership fees which you pay

by direct debit. You can always join the organization again when you're better off. At one point I was paying membership fees not only to Equity but to the Writers' Guild, the Science Fiction Writers of America, the British Fantasy Society, the Society of Woman Writers and Journalists, Fitness Professionals, the Association of Exercise Teachers, the Aerobic Fitness Association of America, the Aberdeen Businesswoman's Club, the Chamber of Commerce and the International Dance Exercise Association. When I added it up it came to an astounding £455.00 per year. For this I got loads of newsletters which I hadn't time to read, containing special offers which I couldn't afford to buy and advertising over-priced workshops which I hadn't time to attend. Check out that you're not doing something similar.

2. Check, too, that you aren't over-insured. Shop around for cheaper house, contents, car, life and health insurance. It's amazing the savings you can make – not to mention all the clock radios, illuminated key rings and travelling bags you'll accumulate in special offers and can recycle as Christmas presents.

3. And, finally, check that you're not paying for your credit card. If yours charges a yearly fee, change it. Credit card companies already make quite enough interest as it is. They are also becoming extremely competitive. Look out for special offers and choose one which doesn't charge a fee and which has the lowest APR. Some companies even give cash incentives for balance transfers.

Ways to Avoid Making Things Worse

1. Contact the experts, the National Debt Helpline (see Useful Addresses).

2. Don't take out loans to repay loans. And *never* borrow from a loan shark.

3. Don't run up bills on credit cards. No matter how desperate you are, never buy anything on a card if the money isn't in the pipeline to pay for it. What you can use them for is to give yourself five to six weeks' leeway. Put the cash for the purchase in your deposit account and get a bit of interest on it. Pay your card off each month so you don't have to pay interest on that. Make your money work for you, no matter how small the amount.

4. Don't borrow money from friends – unless you want to lose your friends.

Survival Strategy 5
Cut-Price Cookery

Forget convenience foods. Overpriced and overpackaged, they are extremely bad value. If you can't afford to go out any more, you might as well spend some of the time at your disposal in the kitchen making healthy casseroles from cheap cuts of meat and/or plenty of filling root vegetables. Cooking can be wonderfully relaxing and therapeutic. Cutting and chopping and slicing. If you are *really* into it and have the time, you could make your own jam and bread and chutney for a quarter of shop prices and have wonderful homemade goodies to give people for presents at Christmas. Anyone, from nine to ninety, would be happy to get a box of homemade fudge in their stocking.

If the kids won't give you peace to cook, involve them. Much better for them than watching *Power Rangers*. Cooking is a wonderful, nurturing social skill which will stand them in very good stead when they're grown. Especially if they're boys. Any child of any age can produce something edible (not those tuna and sweetcorn concoctions they show on *Blue Peter*). I taught my son to measure and shake a salad dressing in a coffee jar when he was only two. People ate it and praised him and he was hooked. When he was old enough to deal with heat (supervised, of course), he started to make pasta sauces and pâtés and such. As I write he is about to start a course at Prue Leith's Cookery School which will qualify him as a professional chef. Watch out Floyd!

Here are some ideas for economical meals:

A friend of mine tells me that, when her husband was a young, poorly paid naval officer she used to virtually feed him on **bacon bits** which were on permanent offer at the grocers. She made bacon and potato hotpot, spaghetti alla carbonara, eggs benedict, bacon and egg flan, bacon and onion pasties and BLTs. He thought she was a wonderful cook and never knew the difference. Inflation has hit the bacon bits, as it has everything else. But you can still get them at the supermarket, and they are still pretty cheap.

Chicken is a healthy option and can be stretched to go a long way. I would reckon to get four meals for four people out of a medium-sized chicken:

Day 1: Roast with all the trimmings.

Day 2: Cold with salad, the American way. Lots of salad and thin strips of chicken and cheese layering the top. Bacon bits, too, if you have any!

Day 3: A choice of . . .
    Fricassee and rice.
    Chicken, lettuce and tomato double-deckers with chips.
    Curry (using a supermarket sauce) and rice.
    Chinese (sweet and sour) and noodles.
    Diced with lettuce and cucumber, tossed in prawn cocktail sauce and piled into hot pitta bread.
    Diced with broccoli and thick white sauce and wrapped in savoury pancakes.

Day 4: Chicken soup, made with the carcass. Any dried up bits of meat left clinging to it after four days will miraculously rehydrate in the stock. Add vegetables, legumes, pasta and/or barley. With crusty bread and a hunk of cheese this makes a delicious main meal and there's usually enough left over for starters the next day.

All of the above also apply to Christmas turkey, of which there is inevitably too much left over.

Alter the balance of your meals. Lots of carbohydrate and a little meat (or veg or legumes if you are a vegetarian): rather than the other way round. Choices include:

- Spaghetti with bolognese sauce (obviously), alla carbonara, marinara, with pesto or whatever takes your fancy. Vary this by getting different pasta shapes. Bows and big fat fettucine (especially the multi-coloured kind) are more appealing and user-friendly to kids than the unmanageable thin sort.

- Kebabs and rice.

- Pizza (make your own) and salad.

- Stews and casseroles (with succulent suet dumplings) made from cheaper cuts of meat (stewing lamb or stewing steak or, as in cassoulet, bits of everything including sausages and butter beans). Heavy on the veg such as turnips and carrots. Served with mounds of mash or rice, or buckwheat or polenta for a change. Use extra potatoes for thickening the sauce.

    A really warming stew can be made with ham-hock and lentils. Another variation is three sorts of dried beans (butter, chickpeas and red kidney) with only a bone for flavouring. (Tell the butcher it's for the dog!)

- Half a pound of mince, on its own or bulked up with soya substitute, will make all sorts of things, not only the aforementioned spaghetti bolognese but stuffed peppers, meatballs, chilli, moussaka, *real* burgers (bind together with egg and add chopped onion), mince pie, mince and tatties (mashed potatoes) with bashed neeps (mashed swede) and stovies (a Scottish concoction the consistency of porridge made of boiled cubed potatoes mixed with mince and gravy and a dash of oatmeal – really sticks to the ribs on a raw November day in the Highlands.

- Not so awful offal. A tub of chicken livers makes a sumptuous risotto alla mamma. Black pudding is a luxury eaten the French way with puréed potatoes and apples fried in butter (thank you, Sophie Grigson). Haggis is tasty. Cumberland sausages are great with red cabbage. Devilled kidneys and liver *au poivre* (rolled in crushed peppercorns and lightly fried) are delicious, nutritious and cheap. Pigs' liver tastes nutty, lambs' kidneys are sweet. People who say they don't like them don't know what they're missing. Liver is high in iron and most offal has virtually zero fat.

- Veggies. Forget the nut cutlets. Think instead of leek and potato soup, baked potatoes and cheese, salads (Caesar, walnut and blue cheese, niçoise), macaroni cheese with tomatoes, French onion soup, quiches and flans using anything fresh in season.

- Nursery food. Rice or bread pudding, toad in the hole, apple crumble and custard. Eggie soldiers. French toast (makes two eggs feed three people for breakfast!). And, talking of breakfast, forget about proprietary brands of cereals. Most are loaded with sugar and very bad value for money. Good old porridge is cheap and cheerful and provides internal central heating on cold winter mornings (add honey and cream for a special treat on high days and holidays).

- Left-overs. Never throw anything out (unless it's past its sell-by date). Less than fresh vegetables make good potage (cooked and puréed in the blender). Bubble and squeak (cold cabbage and potatoes fried up, great with the ubiquitous bacon bits), shepherd's pie and rissoles used to be firm family favourites which make a little go a long way.

I never measure and weigh things. I don't own kitchen scales. My mother, who is a superb pastry-cook, does it all by hand and eye. She measures out flour with a battered old tablespoon – one heaped spoonful equals an ounce. Two dessertspoons comes to the same thing.) Other handy measures:

- A mug holds around half a pint of milk.
- Half a coffee jar of rice will feed two people.
- A full coffee jar of pasta will feed two.
- Look at the amount of contents in the packet (or jar or tin) and measure what you need accordingly, i.e. if the recipe calls for 100 grams and the container weighs 500, judge a fifth of the contents. QED.

The recipes below are working recipes for people who don't care to keep consulting cookbooks.

Chicken Fricassee

Ingredients
1. Long-grained rice: half a mugful for two people.
2. Twice as much water as rice (measure from the same mug) and a splash for good measure.
3. A chicken stock cube.
4. A dash of dried mixed herbs.
5. Cold chicken. Judge this on the amount available, the number and size of the diners and how greedy they are. Generally the meat from a wing will do one, a leg two and a breast three – if this seems measly remember there are other things going in.
6. One medium onion.

7. Two mushrooms per person.
8. Oil.
9. 1 oz butter or margarine.
10. 1 tablespoon flour. (If you want a thicker sauce add a little more but don't make it too glutinous as we'll be putting in extra ingredients.)
11. ½ pint milk. Quarter of a litre is roughly half a pint.
12. Small packet frozen peas.
13. Seasoning to taste.

Method

Wash the rice and place in a saucepan with the water and the stock cube and a dash of dried herbs to make the whole thing look appetizing. Put the lid on, bring to the boil, then simmer until the water has been absorbed and the rice is cooked through. (Twenty minutes for white rice, forty for brown). Try not to peek.

Divide the chicken into bite-sized pieces, chop the onion, slice the mushrooms.

Put a dollop of oil in a frying pan and add the onion and mushrooms. Allow them to sweat over a low heat for five minutes.

Meanwhile, melt the butter in a saucepan and stir in the flour to make a roux. Add the milk gradually, stirring with a wooden spoon to make sure the sauce doesn't go lumpy. If it does go lumpy, beat it with an egg whisk and all will be well.

To this thick, creamy base add the onion and mushrooms, the chicken and the small packet of frozen peas.

Sprinkle on salt and pepper to taste.

Cook through thoroughly (five or six minutes). By this time the rice should be ready.

Serve on warmed plates, rice down one side, fricassee down the other.

Risotto alla mamma

Ingredients

1. Risotto rice.
2. A chicken stock cube.
3. Water as required (about ¾ of a pint).
4. Oil.
5. A medium onion.
6. Two mushrooms per person.
7. Small packet frozen peas.
8. Seasoning to taste.
9. ½ teaspoon dried oregano.
10. 8-oz tub chicken livers (for four people). If you are less than four, then any remaining chicken livers can be used as a scrumptious omelette filling.
11. A knob of butter or margarine.
12. Two ounces hard cheese. (Cheese that has dried out and would normally be thrown away is great for this.)

Method

Wash the rice and put it in a large frying pan with the water and stock cube. Cover and place over a low heat.

Sweat the onion and mushrooms in oil as in the previous recipe and add to the rice mixture.

Five or six minutes before the rice is ready (allow half an hour) stir in the frozen peas and add salt, pepper and a dash of oregano.

Now cook the chicken livers in a knob of butter or margarine and a slosh of oil, turning once. NB Don't overcook. There is nothing as unappetizing as leathery liver. A couple of minutes each side is plenty.

Measure the rice out in little mounds on separate serving plates. Top with the chicken livers and their juices. Sprinkle with grated cheese and pop under the grill until the cheese melts and runs over the dish like golden lava.

Serve immediately.

French Onion Soup

Ingredients

1. One large onion per person.
2. One vegetable stock cube per four onions.
3. Two pints of water per four onions. (Remember a mug equals half a pint. So a mugful for each onion should be just about right.)
4. One piece of thick bread per person.
5. Enough grated cheese for a thick layer on each slice.
6. Seasoning to taste.

Method

Chop the onions and put into a large saucepan with the water and stock cube. (You can sweat the onions in a little oil first if you like, but I find it makes the soup a little greasy.)

Bring to the boil then simmer for half an hour or until the onions are soft.

Toast the bread. Grate the cheese. Cover the toast with the cheese.

Season the soup to taste, then divide into warm fireproof soup bowls. Float a cheesy toast island on each one. Pop under the grill until the cheese has melted.

Eat straight away. Be *very* careful: there is nothing as hot as hot cheese!

Make enough for one serving only. Onion soup tends to go slimy if left overnight.

11 • Financial Fitness: Part II

Eleven Ways to Balance the Books

To update Mr Micawber, 'Annual income £10,000, annual expenditure £9,999, result: happiness. Annual income £10,000, annual expenditure £10,001, result: misery.'

So, how do you adjust when there's more going out than coming in? How do you put off the evil day without losing financial credibility?

If you are a working girl, used to balancing your own books, you may not need any of the following advice. However, if you've been until now a truly dependent woman, whose husband paid all the bills, here are a few simple hints on how to keep your financial head above water in the short and the long term.

1. Where does the money go?

When in doubt, make a list, as ever. No need for expensive ledger books, a school jotter will do. Rule a line down the centre of the first page. List all current outgoings on one side with the exact amounts involved, where known (otherwise put an estimate based on last year's bills plus 10 per cent – nothing ever goes down). Start with those items which involve the biggest outlay – mortgage or rent, rates (house and water), fuel and phone bills, car (petrol, insurance, maintenance), bus and rail fares – and move down through food and household accounts, pocket money (for children *and* adults), postage and papers, school bills (whether your offspring is being educated privately or going through the state system, there always seem to be plenty of these!), pets, hobbies, entertainment, unexpected emergencies, and, last but not least, savings. Don't leave *anything* out.

2. Where does the money come from?
One annual income will simplify things. Just fill that amount in on the other side of the page. Add any extras such as family allowances and/or pensions. Now add up both columns and you will get a general, overall view of your financial state. At this point, *don't panic*.

3. Call a council of war.
Even if one member of the family (you) deals with all the bills, it is only common courtesy to inform everyone if the state of the family exchequer makes it necessary to cancel the weekly comic and the morning rag. Similarly, should you have the sort of household where Dad's wages used to go on necessities and Mum's on luxuries, it will make the loss of the family fortnight in Spain easier to bear if you can point out that unless people turn off the lights and the telly when there's no one in the room, any holiday allowance will have to be spent on the electricity bill. If the kids are old enough, explain to them that you're all in this together, and if they want a pair of the latest street-cred trainers at £100.00 a throw, they will have to get themselves a Saturday job.

4. Divide and rule.
Split your original list into three:

List 1 – bills which need to be paid three-monthly, such as heat, light and phone.

List 2 – monthly outgoings – like mortgage and hire purchase commitments.

List 3 – weekly payments such as housekeeping, pocket money, papers and fares.

Deal with list 2 immediately by instructing your bank to pay those items by standing order. That way, you'll never see the money and, theoretically, never miss it.

5. Make your money work for you.

If you are paid monthly, set aside what you need for the first week and put the remainder of your stipend into an instant-access building society account – even your housekeeping. That way, assuming you are taking out a fixed amount weekly, the money you take out during the last week of the month will have been gathering interest for three weeks. Every little helps. Money budgeted for phone and heating bills, on the other hand, could be in there as long as three months. Over a year this can add up to a substantial amount which can be used either for treats (Christmas or birthdays) or left, as savings, to accumulate. When you do pay the bill, pay by cheque and send it by post with a second-class stamp. This will give you at least three days' leeway (and extra interest) before the cheque is presented at the bank and the money is withdrawn from your interest-paying account. With the building societies and banks vying for your custom, you can now get an interest-paying account with a chequebook.

6. Cheat yourself.

If you are paid weekly, or are on the lower end of the average national income scale and never seem to have enough left over for larger items, here's a crafty way to save without even knowing you're doing it. Say your housekeeping allowance is £50.00 per week. Divide that by two and budget to spend £25.00 every *four* days. This gives you an eight-day week. At the end of seven weeks, you will have one whole week's housekeeping (i.e. £50.00) in hand to spend as you will.

7. Decide what is a household expense and what isn't.

Are you paying for food only, or does your weekly outlay include lots of hidden (and unbudgeted for) extras, such as dry-cleaning, postage and cigarettes? If you are having difficulty making ends meet by Thursday, some of these items may have to be diverted into personal allowances. Otherwise you should consider buying wash and wear clothes in the future; writing fewer, but longer, letters; or giving up smoking (much better for you anyway).

8. Learn to differentiate between a 'wish' and a 'want'.

The former is something you'd like to have. The latter is something you really need. In the ecologically aware nineties, moving away from the consumerism of the last three decades makes good economic sense both on a personal and on a global level. Make do and mend rather than throwing away and starting afresh. If you must discard outgrown children's clothes, for example, recoup some of your losses by selling to a 'nearly new' shop or give them to a deserving charity shop such as Oxfam. While you're there see if you can pick up some good nearly news for you and yours. Jumble sales are great for this, too. I once bought a perfectly good school blazer for my son for £1.00. On the food front, rediscover the culinary joys of left-overs in scrumptious recipes such as bread and butter pudding and bubble and squeak (see Survival Strategy 5).

9. Save energy.

Unless you are very old (or very young) and in danger of

succumbing to hypothermia, you can save money (and energy) by the simple expedient of always keeping the central heating a notch below maximum. This will make a calculable difference to your fuel bills and will hardly affect the heat of your home. If you really feel the cold, put on an extra layer of clothes and, if you live alone, live in one room during the winter months. By wearing your clothes twice (not socks or undies), you will use half the energy, half the water, half the washing powder and, theoretically, your clothes should last twice as long. To save time and electricity, don't iron bedlinen (fold instead), do only collars, cuffs and fronts of shirts, press trousers under the mattress. Similarly, thinking, 'Do I need to drive, or would a walk be better for me?' can save on fuel bills. If you take the kids to school every day by car, get together with a few like-minded mums and organize a school rota. Not only will you save money this way, you'll do your bit for the environment by reducing congestion on the roads and protecting the threatened ozone layer.

10. If you are paid in cash or are on a fixed income such as a pension which doesn't warrant a bank or building-society account, **using envelopes** (recycle those from unsolicited mail) marked variously with weekly outgoings (housekeeping, gas, TV stamp, etc.) is a good way of keeping track. Provided you divide the money up as soon as you get back from the Post Office and never rob Peter to pay Paul, you should be able to keep solvent from one week to the next.

11. Should you, Heaven forbid, find yourself incapable of making ends meet, *don't* bury your head in the sand and hope the problem will go away. It won't. Act immediately. Don't run up an overdraft without asking the bank manager first. That will only lead to nasty, threatening letters and more worry. And as I said before, *never* borrow to pay off debts. Seductively worded adverts offering to amalgamate all monies owed and pay them off monthly actually add extra interest and sink you deeper in the mire of insolvency. Instead, tackle one thing at a time. Write letters to all your creditors (building society, HP and credit card companies) and explain the situation. Offer to pay the very most you can afford – after you have deducted your living expenses – until your position improves. Most organizations, given honesty and the facts, will do their best to help restructure your loan repayments to reflect your depleted circumstances. But ignoring creditors could mean repossession of your furniture, your car and, eventually, your home.

The important thing to remember about money is that you don't have to have a degree in accountancy to keep it under control. A little common-sense and forward planning can help you cut through the mystique and keep you, if not in the lap of luxury, at least ahead of the financial game.

12 • Financial Fitness: Part III

Something for Nothing – or almost

It is very rare for a woman to find herself better off financially after a split-up, whatever the popular press would have you believe about star alimony pay-outs. When the necessities have been seen to, there's usually very little, if any, in the way of disposable income left to play with.

Like it or not – it's economy time. But try to adjust your attitude so that you don't end up feeling sorry for yourself. Look on it as a matter of choice rather than necessity. You could persuade yourself – and your friends – that you are merely trying to redress the ecological balance. Once you go down this road you may be surprised at how little you need to get by. And at how your priorities change. And as I said before, having to be 'careful' really heightens your appreciation when you do have a treat. If you only get a Chinese meal on your birthday, I guarantee it will taste twice as good as it did when you could afford to indulge every other week. We are talking quality as opposed to quantity here.

The truth is we all have enormously high expectations of what we deserve in terms of lifestyle these days. We subliminally accept the television-commercial version and tend to think ourselves extremely hard done by if we don't have the best and the latest of everything, from disc-drives to dishwashers. But it is only a couple of generations ago – when I was a child – that central heating was virtually unheard of, foreign holidays were reserved for the rich and not even the rich had a telly. In the war everyone had to tighten their belts. And most of them were a lot healthier for it. Digging allotments and eating the results did wonders for the cholesterol level. A mere century back, nobody had a washing machine or a hoover or a fridge. Life was hard – but it went on. As it will do for you.

However, if you finish up with more month than money, here are some more ways to make ends meet somewhere in the middle.

Bring Back Barter

Money isn't everything, although when you haven't any it may seem like it. People used to barter what they had (goods, services, skills) for what they wanted. You can do the same.

If you have gardening friends, you'll find that they always have a glut of something – more lettuces, strawberries and greens than they can eat. Rather than let them go to waste, swap their excess in return for clothes repairs, baby-sitting or things you make from their raw ingredients (apple pie, strawberry jam).

Before I left Aberdeen I had a great arrangement with a good friend who is a wine shipper. We swapped exercise classes for wine (a luxury I could no longer afford). I slotted her into a class that I was running anyway. She got the wine wholesale. Goods in exchange for services. The quality of both our lives was improved and everybody was happy. And no money changed hands.

If you let a spare room to an alternative practitioner, like a reflexologist or an aromatherapist, you could barter free appointments in their down-time in return for answering the phone for them in their up-time.

Swap skills: cook for a friend who sews or vice versa; clean a flat in return for car maintenance.

Grow Your Own
Even if you aren't a gardener and you don't have a garden, you can start a herb garden on the window-sill, grow mushrooms in the cellar, make yoghurt in the airing cupboard. Turn a sunny bay window into a greenhouse – if you can keep ordinary decorative houseplants alive, you can grow tomatoes and chives. One friend has a satsuma plant in the lounge, with *real* satsumas.

Wish-Books
If you can't afford to buy household items for cash, consider catalogues. You can spread the cost of shopping over several months. Purchases are normally interest-free paid over twenty weeks for small items, or thirty-eight weeks for larger things. You *can* get one-hundred-week terms but you'll have to pay interest on them. You can buy everything from toys to car insurance to a new duvet by monthly instalments (with 10 per cent back in commission). Or you could even run an agency (so you get 10 per cent commission back on everything your friends buy too).

One tip: no matter how much you covet something, never make a purchase when the catalogue first arrives. After a couple of months you can get up to 25 per cent off your initial order in incentives. I did this when I was skint and had to replace the fridge.

Shopping at home has other advantages, too. It saves transport money. You get everything on approval. Free postage (even if you're sending something back). Most of the phone lines are open till 10.00 p.m. so you can shop at your leisure. No screaming kids, no sweaty dressing rooms. You can try your purchase on, away from prying eyes, in a good light, at home, with the relevant accessories. Then you'll know whether the colours really match.

I use catalogues all the time. I loathe shopping but I love getting parcels. Buying from wish-books is like Christmas all year round.

Clothes

These can be the last thing in the equation when you're struggling to cover the basics. But slopping around in old jeans and your ex's discarded rugby sweater can be demoralizing. Get more value for your money by frequenting dress agencies. Look for them in your local *Yellow Pages*. People who wouldn't be seen dead in last season's styles sell to agencies to get back a little of their fashion investment. Consequently the quality of the garments tends to be high. Some even specialize in couture clothes. And if you happen to have a wonderful ball gown in the back of the wardrobe which you know you're never going to wear again, you might get a few bob for it with which to buy something more relevant to your current situation. Like a boiler suit!

Entertainment

Libraries are an under-used free resource. Your local library stocks all the latest bestsellers, newspapers and glossy magazines. Most now stock CDs and tapes. Some in Scotland even stock paintings, so if your man ran off with the Picasso you can fill the space on the wall. They hold regular story readings for kids and play sessions for under-fives. You can get reference books on any subject from crochet to quantum physics. They're also a marvellous place to source other information, such as classes (evening and exercise), courses, support groups, societies and events on offer locally. They generally have a cheap photocopier and if you want a particular book and it's not in stock they can order it for you. If you're a bookaholic, like me, they also hold regular sales of old stock once or twice a year. A trip to the library makes a welcome change from TV.

Should your television conk out and there's no way you can even think of buying a new one, firms like Granada, who hire them out, will often sell ex-hire models very cheap. They may not be the most stylish or up-to-the-minute items, but they work and most have a year's guarantee.

If you think your existence is a disaster, try visiting the local courts one afternoon. All human life is there, and some sad and salutary tales unfold. It is fascinating to watch the wheels of justice turn and if you are of a literary bent, a trip could furnish you with enough material for a novel or a TV series. Now there's a thought.

Entertain someone else. Read to the blind. Drive for the disabled. Volunteer for trips away with older or disadvantaged people. Donate a few hours to delivering papers and chatting to patients in your local hospital. Giving your services to others can be extremely rewarding. It takes your mind off your own problems and focuses you on how lucky you really are.

Hobbies. Remember knitting? It is very therapeutic, especially when you can create a high-fashion garment while watching *Coronation Street*. My own criterion is that the end result should never *look* as though I knitted it myself. Or you could sew, crochet, tat, embroider or make tapestry. Very soothing.

Over sixty? Take advantage of everything going, from bus passes to free chiropody, prescriptions, glasses and teeth. You can get special rates at leisure centres to keep yourself in shape. If there isn't an over-sixties class, ask them to organize one. Meanwhile, swim or get the instructors to show you how to negotiate the machines. Most hairdressers do cheap days for pensioners. Most councils run lunch clubs. Most cinemas and theatres do special prices for senior citizens at matinees.

Under sixty? In some areas, if you are a single parent or on the dole, you can get cut-price entrance fees to council leisure facilities for yourself and/or the children. Enjoyable for the whole family: swimming lessons for the kids, aerobics classes for you to make new friends, get rid of your depression and create the kind of body you've always dreamed of.

Food Shopping

Change from brand names to supermarket specials. The produce is just as good, you just don't get the fancy packaging. You can get cereal, orange juice, bread, beans, washing powder, and many other staples for about half the normal price.

If possible, do your main shop on a Tuesday. Apart from the fact that the queues at the check-out are shorter, you can also get bargains of meat not sold at the weekend. At weekends shop last thing – for give-away prices on perishables like fruit, vegetables, bread, date-stamped produce.

Markets are great for fresh, cheap produce and lip-smacking wet-fish stalls.

Christmas

For the first year, opt out. It is one of the most expensive and, if you're alone, the saddest times of the year.

Don't buy cards. Most people get so many they won't notice if you don't send any for a couple of years – by that time things will have picked up and you will be sending them back, unless you decide to save the rainforest and never send them back. Try an ad in the paper instead: 'Jane Doe wishes all her friends, relations and colleagues . . .' With the cost of cards and postage nowadays this could work out cheaper. An ad looks very grand, and think of the time you save; one phonecall and it's done.

If you're single and alone, tell everyone you're going away (to Hawaii, your mother's, the moon). Then stock up on novels (from the library) and treats (scrambled eggs and smoked salmon offcuts) and stay in bed for a couple of days. Take long baths, meditate, put on face-packs (made from yoghurt with eye-packs of used tea-bags), shave your legs and do your nails. Relax. When you return to circulation you'll be so laid back you'll look as though you have been to Hawaii or maybe your mother's, if not the moon.

Our first Christmas after my partner left, my son and I split up. We'd both decided we couldn't face Christmas in the house. Stevie went to his father's relations in Devon. It was a real Victorian Christmas with party games and all the trimmings and, not only did he love it, it taught him that he hadn't been abandoned by the entire family. I went to my London flat and visited all my old friends there, particularly those who pre-dated my ex. It reminded me that I had had a good life before him. We both returned having had a pleasant break from each other and a much more enjoyable time than if we had stayed home to wallow in memories.

By the second year the Ghost of Christmas Past had been exorcized to the extent that we were able to stay happily at home and build some new memories of our own.

Survival Strategy 6
Affirmations

Affirmations, also called self-talk, are strong positive statements about how things are and how you would like them to be.

We talk to ourselves all the time, we just don't always realize we're doing it. Unfortunately, because a great deal of this stream of consciousness is negative (I'll never get this right; I wish I didn't have to; why does this always happen to me? . . .), it can undermine our confidence and give us an unduly pessimistic and fearful view of life.

Affirmations are a way of redressing the balance.

Most of the mental scribble that besets us through the day is the result of outmoded programming. Things that we were told as a child by our parents or other authority figures (don't touch; naughty girl; you'll never amount to anything; your sister's the pretty one; if you go out of the garden the bogey man will get you). Things which, now that we are responsible grown-ups, are not only irrelevant but absolutely counter-productive. Things which hold us back from realizing our true potential.

How many of us would truly want to go back to being a child? Think of it: no freedom of movement, no disposable income, no control over our lives, obliged to live by someone else's rules . . . Yet some of us have been so indoctrinated that we are still living daily by those rules, long after the controller and the situation has gone. Childhood conditioning can literally stunt your growth. Try to remember this if you have children of your own.

Affirmations are a powerful way of widening our horizons. Just because something has always happened a certain way doesn't mean it always has to happen that way in the future. If it did, we would still be wearing woad and living in caves. Change is movement. Change is growth. Change your perceptions and you can open up your world. Just because you've never been able to swim, or type, or dance, doesn't mean you can't. You have the power to rewrite future history in your head. First by affirming 'I can' (swim or type or dance) and then by going out and taking lessons.

Affirmations are a way to help retrain the mind. Affirmations can open you up to previously unthought-of possibilities, collapse limiting ideas and reinforce your own sense of self-worth.

The things we say to ourselves become our reality. So we might as well make that reality as upbeat, enabling, enjoyable and positive as possible.

Affirmations are a way to create a better truth for yourself. They can be general (the world is a wonderful nurturing place) or specific (I am lovable just as I am). They can be directed to any area of your life from the vital to the trivial. They can make a quantifiable difference to your quality of life.

A couple of theoretical points before we start on the practical applications:

1. Affirmations should always be stated in the present tense: 'I am a successful screenwriter making £100,000 a year,' rather than, 'I'm going to be . . . someday . . . in the dim distant future . . . when I'm probably going to be too old to enjoy it.' The former is a definite statement of fact. The latter is an exercise in hedge-betting. Have the courage of your convictions. Suspend your disbelief. If not now, when?

2. Affirmations should always be stated in the positive. 'I am now eating only those foods which energize and strengthen my body,' rather than, 'I must *not* eat chocolate.' Move towards the good rather than away from the bad. Eventually so much good will flow into your life, the bad will be eased out to make space.

Now, here are some headings each with an example of an affirmation to give you an idea. Read through these and then try to construct some personal affirmations of your own. Don't make a big thing about it. The first, most spontaneous idea is probably the best. There may be some areas of your life with which you are perfectly happy. That is an affirmation in itself – one which perhaps you hadn't even thought of.

You may think of lots of affirmations for one area, only one for another. You may draw a complete blank. If you can't think of anything, don't force it, set the book aside and forget the whole thing. Some time during the day (or night) when you're least expecting it, an affirmation will pop into your mind. Write it down. It will probably start a torrent of thoughts from which you can pick and choose. Feel free to think of totally different categories.

Health
'I will always look and feel young and healthy.'

Wealth
'I always have everything I need, when I need it.'

The Pursuit of Happiness
'I am happy to be me.'

Body
'My body is in excellent shape. I am strong and active.'

Mind
'My mind is opening up to new exciting ideas.'

Emotions
'I am secure in my ability to deal with life's challenges.'

Spirituality
'The universe provides.'

Relationships
'I am attracting the perfect loving relationship into my life.'

Home
'I live in a comfortable environment where I can relax and feel secure.'

Job or career
'I enjoy my work and am well paid for it.'

Weight
'I maintain my perfect weight easily and effortlessly.'

Self-image
'I am comfortable with myself and always look my best.'

Travel
'I have the time and money to take whatever breaks I need.'

Friends
'I have many wonderful, supportive friends.'

Creativity
'I am full of creative ideas which I put into practice.'

You can be even more specific than this with your affirmations. The more you put in the more you're likely to manifest. Have fun with it. Dream big or you might as well not bother.

Inspire yourself enough and you're more likely to get up the head of steam you need to turn your dream into a reality.

What to Do with Your Affirmations

1. Put them in places you can see them often.

2. Read them aloud . . . in front of a mirror . . . with conviction!

3. Allow them to circulate in your head in down time, such as when you're stuck in a traffic jam. Much better for the blood-pressure than road-rage.

4. Keep them to yourself. It only takes one person saying, 'Ah ha. Still haven't got the Mercedes, I see,' to knock you right off base and start you thinking perhaps your dreams are silly.

Dreams are *never* silly. And they're free. So . . .

1. Get a pack of 6" x 5" cards and write one of your favourite affirmations on each. Then place them in appropriate positions around the house. 'I am now my perfect weight' could be stuck on the fridge door. Place 'I am successful' on top of the word-processor. Tack 'I am attracting the perfect man' above your bed. You get the picture?

2. Make a motivating tape to play in the car on the way to a meeting, on the drive back from dropping the kids at school, or on your headset on the tube – quietly, please.

3. Write affirmations on the back of used envelopes (save the rain-forest!) and tuck them in your diary or journal or use them as book-marks. If you are a doodler add illustrations.

4. Take this a stage further and make a treasure map or

collage of your favourite, most immediate affirmation. Suppose this is 'I have a beautiful new home'. Draw the home, furnish it (with items cut out of a magazine if you're no artist), colour it in, add details as you think of them. Cut out a picture of yourself and place it in the frame, add the kids, draw in a new man if you want one.

Vocal affirmations are strong. Writing them down engages more of your energy and makes them stronger. Treasure maps are the most powerful of all. They are like a template for the future. The very act of creating one is therapeutic in itself. And they draw all kinds of energy to them. Once you've completed your work of art, stick it on a wall where you'll see it often. Or fold it up and carry it in your handbag so that you can look at it on the way to that important interview. Allow the image to inspire you. Then bounce into your meeting and see what happens.

5. Use the image of your treasure map to boost your creative visualization sessions.

A few observations on affirmations:

Expect manifestations to come from directions you hadn't anticipated.

Approach the whole thing in a state of childlike anticipation, as though it's Christmas Eve and you *know* Santa is going to deliver the goods.

Keep the greed in check. When you were a child if you asked for a dolls' house and a Cindy doll and a nurse's outfit and a pony all in one year you were probably disappointed.

Relax. Just release the affirmation, the wish, the prayer, the intent into the ether and let the universe take care of it.

Be flexible. If it, or something like it, doesn't materialize, don't feel defeated. Perhaps, deep down, you didn't really want it after all. Or maybe the time's not right yet. Or maybe what you wanted wouldn't be good for you. Or maybe something better is going to happen.

Acknowledge your successes. When something manifests itself savour it, enjoy it, be delighted with it – and with yourself. Affirm that your affirmations worked.

13 • Do You Sincerely Want Another Man?

It's what you bring to a relationship that's important, not what you take out. But straight after an abandonment you tend to be so needy that all you have to bring is your desperation.

You are in a state of shell-shock. One of the symptoms of this is panic. You can't make a decision, even a minor one, without breaking into a cold sweat. What you want more than anything is for someone wonderful to come along and 'take you away from all this'. To love you, protect you, wrap you up in cotton wool and assume the awesome responsibility of organizing your life. To kiss you and make it better.

This is not a sensible frame of mind in which to go in search of a new partner.

Abandoned women are notoriously exploitable and it's a sad fact that not every man who offers affection at this point has your best interests at heart. In short, you are fair game for any unscrupulous sleaze-hound who pays court. And if you fall for a con man's chat, and he lets you down, you'll only have yourself to blame.

You are even more vulnerable to nice but thoroughly unsuitable wimps who may well bore you to death six months down the line. After a break-up you may be grateful for anyone but if a man doesn't *add* something to your life which you can't give yourself – and that includes sex, tender loving care, money, friendship, support and/or joy – then why put up with the snoring and the socks?

We are all looking for love. But most of us are looking in the wrong place. There are degrees of love, and sexual obsession is only a very small part of the equation (although, bombarded as we are with sex in movies and commercials, you'd be forgiven for thinking it was the entire picture). Love is a universal, all-enveloping concept. It involves not only loving your partner but your children, your family, friends, pets, plants, the environment, the whole planet. It also involves loving yourself. And the best way to get love is to give it. To any of the above.

Romance is wonderful. It fills your body with adrenalin and makes you feel (and look) ten years younger. But, to be cynical, it's the hook that draws us into the reality of child-bearing and child-rearing. Like the Roman's bread and circuses, sexual love is the organism's way of perpetuating itself while distracting us from what's *really* going on. For hundreds of years we've been buying into the chivalric myth of the knight in shining armour. Why? Because we *want* it to be true.

At the beginning of a love affair we project all kinds of heroic attributes on to the beloved. He's the best, the most, the cleverest, the handsomest. Even his faults are turned to his advantage. If he drinks, it's because nobody understands him (except you, of course); if he gets the sack it's because the boss doesn't appreciate his exceptional talents. He is perfect in every respect. And the things that aren't quite perfect can be changed by the love of a good woman. Does this sound familiar?

Time goes on and he doesn't respond to our attempts to change him. Nor does he live up to the superhuman image we have charged him with.

And here's the topper. Usually we haven't even told him

Do You Sincerely Want Another Man?

what that image is. No, I'm not trying to elicit sympathy for the man who 'done you wrong'. What I am saying is that blokes are only human. We need to give them a clue about what it is that we want. If they can't, won't or don't give it, we then need to decide – are we willing to make do with less – or cut our losses and leave?

Like they did!

A society based on the couple is a very hard one to sustain. The stress is so concentrated. We are expected to be all things to each other. It's a concept so doomed to failure that it's a miracle it ever works out.

It has not always been thus. Stone Age man hunted, Stone Age woman planted and gathered. Socially, the men congregated in one cave (to drink, boast and throw dice). The women did likewise – in the cave next door (to eat, gossip and make quilts). They only came together for sex. When the hormones had died down they hardly had to see each other. So there was less chance of them getting on each other's nerves.

Other societies also worked out more durable templates. The Maoris had a wonderful scheme (it may still be going on) where the younger members worked and procreated and the older generation, with more time and patience at their disposal, brought up the children. This seems to me a solution that is much more sensible than subjecting a couple who are just getting their own relationship worked out to the pressures of producing and supporting a family. The Maori way, the young got laid, the children got loved and the old didn't get discarded. Nobody was trying to do so many things at once that they ended up doing nothing right.

OK. So say none of this has persuaded you; say you're still desperate for another bloke. What are the options?

1. Other people's husbands.

2. Toy boys.

3. Father figures.

4. Dead-beats.

5. Dead-heads.

6. Genuine prospects.

Let's take them one at a time.

1. **Other people's husbands.** If you are young and sexy, prepare for them to be round in droves. The theory is, you're alone so you must be desperate. Even if you're neither young nor sexy, you might be unpleasantly surprised. The insensitivity of it is almost unbelievable. As though you would deliberately put a friend through the kind of agony you've been suffering. You wouldn't, would you? No matter how desperate you are, OPHs should be a complete no-no. Be prepared for them to be devious. They will tell you their wife doesn't understand them, they don't sleep together, they always found you madly desirable. Clap-trap. What they want is to get their end away with no strings attached. Because of the nature of the liaison they won't even take you out. They'll creep round to your place at their own convenience. The whole thing will be conducted in a state of sordid secrecy. Ask yourself: what's in it for you?

2. **Toy boys.** Good for a brief fling and to prove that you are still attractive, but impractical as a long-term prospect. Young men, bless their hearts, tend to be very self-centred and quite inexperienced in bed. And there's usually no frame of reference. You have to have something to talk about after the event and if he's too young to know who Humphrey Bogart is . . . Finally

there's your image to consider. When an older man gets embroiled with a younger woman no one blinks, but even in today's enlightened climate, a mature woman with a toy boy on her arm is seen more as a figure of fun than an object of envy. There's always the underlying implication that you're paying for it. And, since young men seldom have any money, you may well be.

3. **Father figures.** If you're suddenly attracted to a much older man (and you've never been before), he's probably a security figure. If he's attractive, loaded and treats you like gold dust, great. But do you really want to spend the rest of your life listening to the Archers and being sensible?

4. **Dead-beats.** There is always a woman somewhere desperate enough to take in any stray or cast-off, no matter how unappetizing they may be. What you need at the moment is *less* responsibility, not more. Until you know what you really want.

5. **Dead-heads.** Some spare men are spare for a reason. They are dysfunctional in some way: they're addicted or paranoid or violent. They may be manic depressives or have Oedipus complexes or just want a meal-ticket. If a guy seems too good to be true, he probably is.

6. **Genuine prospects.** Thin on the ground but out there. For the first time in living memory there are more men than women per head of the population, so if you're serious about it you *can* find one. Unfortunately dating doesn't get any easier the second time around. If you've just been rejected, it can be very scary to subject yourself to a situation where you may be rejected again. But you'll never find another man

sitting at home. You have to take your courage in both hands and get out into the market-place.

So where do you start?

Dating Agencies

These are no longer the last refuge of what my teenage son refers to as 'sad bastards'. With increasing urban alienation they are sometimes the only channel through which busy people with demanding jobs can meet their peers. There are all kinds of dating agencies from the generic computer sort which deals with all ages and socio-economic groups, to the more specialized types which stick to a particular section of the market (graduates, career people, over-fifties). Some offer a luxury service where they personally vet each client and genuinely try to match them with someone compatible. Others work on the lucky dip principle that if they set you up with ten people, there's bound to be *one* you get on with. You pays your money and you takes your choice. Most agencies are respectable these days (though, by the very nature of the business, there's bound to be the odd rogue lurking around). They are supposed to be registered and regulated by certain guidelines. Some are better than others. None of them can guarantee results.

Where do you find them? Look out for ads in the national and daily papers, in women's magazines, or, for specialized agencies, in target magazines (*Choice*, *Active Life* if you're older; ecological periodicals if you hanker after a New Age partner) and good old *Yellow Pages*.

How do you separate the wheat from the chaff? Do a bit of preliminary paperwork. Make a list of relevant agencies from the above sources. Now call each of them. If you like the sound of the person on the other end of the phone, make an appointment to see them. If their people skills leave something to be desired (if they are indifferent, pushy or obvious salespeople), scrub them off. Of those remaining, ask what their terms are. If they hedge, scrub them off as well – you probably can't afford them. If they are up-front but too expensive for your pocket, say so. You can keep them on file in expectation of better times to come. By now your list should have shrunk to a manageable size. Go and see each of these possibilities in turn.

Between the phone call and the interview, decide what kind of partner you're looking for. It's the first thing they'll ask and it's as well to be prepared. If you want a forty-year-old history professor with a good body, a kind face and £40,000 a year, write it down. (If you want a twenty-year-old Chippendale lookalike, ditto – just don't hold your breath, is all.) Decide which of these elements, if any, you're willing to compromise on. If he had dogs, kids or an ageing parent living in, would it matter? What, in Hollywood-agent parlance, is the deal-breaker? If they have nobody on their books who remotely tallies with your idea of an ideal mate, then it may be best to look elsewhere. If you lower your sights at this point who knows what you may end up with.

At the interview you'll be able to tell by the location of the offices, the general atmosphere and the personality of the interviewer whether you are going to be comfortable with the company. If you're not (taking into account the nervousness you'll undoubtedly feel at the strangeness of the situation), then you should make your excuses and leave. Never part with any money until you're absolutely sure.

The next hurdle is the forms. When filling them in – be honest. Don't try to make yourself out to be something you're not in order to try to snag a better mate. Preferable that people should be pleasantly surprised than the other way round.

On the first date, be sensible. Dress appropriately. A décolleté blouse or a skirt cut up to your bum is bound to give the wrong impression, as is lots of make-up. Don't dress down either. If you're glamorous by nature, don't wear a brown suit and flatties. Try to be yourself. If you don't think that's good enough, how can you expect anyone else to? Arrange to meet somewhere neutral and unthreatening. A hotel bar, where a woman can sit unmolested if her date happens to be late, is better than a noisy pub. And stay sober even if you're terrified. If your date is late, it's likely he's terrified too. Men don't find this kind of thing any easier than women. In self-defence have an excuse ready in case it's a total disaster — a believable one that won't leave the man with egg on his face. Needless to say, in this age of Aids it would be foolish in the extreme to go to bed with someone on the first date.

Personal Columns

You can put an ad in the personal column of your local newspaper or in magazines such as *Time Out*. Your anonymity will be respected so there's no need to worry about weirdos ringing you up at three o'clock in the morning. Anyone wishing to reply has to write to a box number. This gives you an opportunity to separate the good from the bad (ask for a photo if you're concerned about the ugly). I know a perfectly ordinary young working girl who took out an ad and got forty replies in the next post. On the other hand I know a man who got none. By reading the relevant messages you will get a flavour of the type of person who patronizes such small ads. The columns are all quite different in terms of the contributors they attract. Some are very weird indeed.

Good luck.

Singles Bars

Good in theory, not so good in practice. Often frequented by just the sort of lounge lizard you should avoid like the plague. If you *do* go, go mob-handed, with lots of girlfriends as camouflage. On the other hand, if you have a penchant for medallion man . . .

Dining Clubs

These have been springing up all over and most large towns now have one. For a yearly fee you'll be given the opportunity to dine out, in pleasant restaurants, with people of like mind and similar background. You pay extra for the meal, of course, but the charge for this, which varies according to restaurant and area, usually includes welcome drinks and half a bottle of wine. The dinners are hosted by a member of staff, hired for their social skills, who is there to do the introductions, keep the ball rolling and fill in any awkward silences. They operate a strict equal numbers policy so you don't end up with ten women and two men; after you've paid your joining fee you are at liberty to attend as few, or as many, nights out as you choose.

Some dining clubs (like Great Company, based in London with branches in Bristol and Manchester) also organize singles holidays both at home and abroad and since all the participants are on their own, they don't include the iniquitous single supplement usually charged by other tour operators. They also do themed weekends (golf, walking, wine-tasting, murder).

Dining out seems to me to be a most civilized way to meet people. The number involved is small enough so there's a chance you'll remember some names, and good food and wine are great relaxers. Of course if you get seated next to a terminal bore, it could be a very long night.

If you are short of money but have social skills yourself,

you might like to offer your services to a dining club as a host – you'll not only meet people, you'll also get paid for it.

If there isn't a club in your area, why not start one?

Other Places to Meet Men

If you're a business person, join the local **Chamber of Commerce**. It has a ratio of 90 per cent male members and lots of functions.

Evening Classes. Car maintenance has a ratio of 99 per cent men.

Job as a barmaid. Can be convivial if you choose your venue. 'Cheers' rather than the 'Dog and Ferret'. But ask yourself – do you want a boyfriend who spends all his leisure hours drinking Fosters?

Sports' clubs. You have a reason to be there (to get in shape) so it doesn't look as though you're on a man-hunt (very off-putting). Again choose carefully. There are leisure centres and there are sweat-boxes (gyms). In a fitness club opt for weight training (mostly guys), not classes (mostly girls). Prepare to be disappointed, though. The Schwarzenegger lookalike pumping iron may be more interested in his own body than yours. The few guys in aerobic dance classes are probably more interested in each other.

Dance classes. Ballroom, salsa or line dancing. Look in the local papers for classes in your area. A great way to meet friends and have fun. And, at about £3.00 an hour, it won't break the bank.

Finally, tell all your friends you're now available. Maybe they have brothers, cousins, uncles who are just waiting for a nice girl like you to come along? Maybe their husband has a single partner, boss, business associate who'd be just right for you? Stranger things have happened.

Incidentally, don't be surprised if some of your girlfriends become inexplicably cool. If their own marriages are on the rocky side, your very presence may make them uncomfortable. Not just because they may not trust you with their own partners but also because your situation threatens their psychological security and holds up a mirror into which they would rather not look.

Avoid cruises and cookery courses. The chance of finding an available man on any of these is minimal.

If you're looking for an escort, with no strings attached, gay friends can be lifesavers. Sensitive, compassionate, generous and understanding, they are wonderful allies. Most are witty, stylish and tremendous fun to be with. If you're still too brittle to get involved with a heterosexual man, you can enjoy a night out in a gay friend's company without worrying about the 'jump' at the end of the meal. Best of all, they never censure if you behave badly or burst into tears over the fish course.

Ditto sons. Mine kept me from going crazy by inviting me out for the occasional half with his mates (now *there's* a compliment).

If you are in the position where you are being pursued by someone you're not interested in, better to say 'no' than let yourself in for an evening which you know is going to culminate in wrestling in the car on the way home. A bag of chips in front of the telly is a more positive choice than going out with someone you don't like for the sake of a free meal.

Sex and the single girl
If you have no luck with the above and you feel you're getting desperately out of practice, don't panic. Sex is like riding a bike – once you've mastered the technique, you never lose it. All it needs is for the right person to come along and press the appropriate buttons.

Meanwhile, pamper yourself. Discover the joys of peace in bed. Read, eat, watch sad movies and cry. Give yourself time. Above all, don't despair. Virtual reality sex-suits will be with us any day now!

14 • Connections

One of the more unpleasant side-effects of abandonment is self-obsession. You're not tuned in to anything except your own misery. You become totally oblivious to other people's problems, feelings or opinions. You ask for advice only to ignore it. You interrupt if the subject changes to something other than you. You don't really hear what anyone is saying, you're just waiting for a lull in the conversation so you can start moaning again. Every chance encounter becomes an excuse to replay the record of your grievances over and over and over again.

Friends and acquaintances are alternately shunned (you don't answer the phone, pretend you're out when the doorbell rings, cross the road to avoid them) or used (as sounding-boards, sympathy-givers, sponges to mop up your latest vitriol).

This can be very wearing on the innocent bystander. Especially if they are being asked to take sides. At a time when you need all the genuine support you can get, you are in danger of alienating yourself from the very people that you need most. Unless you recognize what you're doing and modify your behaviour, you'll find your friends will gradually disappear until you're left talking to the wall.

The way out of this self-defeating maze is, first, to become aware of what you're doing and, second, to begin to look out rather than in. Start to listen again rather than simply talk. Try to focus on someone else for a change. In other words, learn to reconnect.

It can be a long process. Self-obsession is a hard habit to break. The most effective way to tackle it is to take it one step at a time.

Start by acknowledging what you're doing. Have a standby phrase handy so that you can extricate yourself each time you catch yourself going into moan-mode. 'That's enough about me. What's life like with you?' – or something like that.

Try to really listen to what the other person is telling you. Listen for its own sake, not just so you can compare whatever they say with something which has happened to you. 'Isn't that just like a man? I remember when so and so did just the same . . . ' and you're off again.

You could time yourself, i.e. resolve to get through five minutes of a meeting without mentioning your ex. Next time make it ten, then twenty. At a lunch date do it by the course. Not a word until the soup has been cleared away. Next time try to make it through the entrée. Once you get as far as the coffee without broaching the subject, you know you've cracked it.

One day in the future, when someone asks you how you are, you'll be astounded to discover that you're able to say, 'Much better,' and leave it at that.

This doesn't mean you should be afraid to ask for help when you need it. As long as it's something specific you want and not just endless sympathy, most people are happy to oblige. When I decided to make ends meet by turning the dining-room into a guestroom and taking in a lodger, everyone rallied round. One friend came and painted the walls. Other friends donated a single bed, a lamp, a small wardrobe, a chest of drawers, bedding. Most of these bits and pieces were stored in attics or garages. Those who offered felt good passing them on. And I ended up with a lettable room.

What you shouldn't do is behave like an emotional vampire, draining goodwill and giving nothing in return. If you ask for help, either pay back the favour in kind (straight away so you don't forget) or, if it's a skill (like changing the oil in the car), watch what's going on so that you can do it yourself next time. You're a grown-up. Once you've been shown how to do something, there's no reason, other than laziness, why you shouldn't do it yourself.

George Bernard Shaw said that the true joy of life is 'being a force of nature instead of a feverish selfish little clod of ailments and grievances complaining that the world will not devote itself to making you happy'. Be a force of nature not a selfish little clod. Start connecting again. Not for what you can get out of it, but for what you can put in.

Here are some ideas to get you started:

- **Call a halt.** Ring your friends, thank them for their support and ask them if there's anything you can do for them in return. Be prepared to *do* it.

- **Open up.** If you've been hiding the awful truth from your mother (because you don't want to worry her or because she said it wouldn't work), drop your pride and go home for a long weekend. Mothers know how to kiss and make it better whatever age you are.

- **Give a little.** Rework relationships in your extended family. If you've been neglecting Great-Aunt Marjorie, now's the time to pay her a visit. And try to make peace with your inlaws, especially if you have children. Whatever their son did to you is not their fault and they may be as appalled by his behaviour as you are.

- **Push back social barriers.** Get to know your neighbours in the street or the block. Christmas is a good time for this. If you're feeling isolated, drop a dozen cards in adjacent letter-boxes saying you're having open house on Christmas Eve or whatever. Mulled wine and mince-pies won't break the bank and could open up a whole new support system. If there's an older, more isolated person living nearby, you could give them a hand by offering them a lift to the supermarket or transporting heavy items like potatoes. You don't have to turn into Mary Poppins overnight. Just realize that the best way to get attention, or affection, or love, is to *give* it.

- **Help yourself.** Look in the *Yellow Pages* for self-help groups. If you're a single parent, Gingerbread has branches all over the country. Your local church can be a genuine source of connection, as can community centres which have all kinds of activities going on. Pop down and have a look on their notice-board. Join your area Neighbourhood Watch. Somebody has to do it.

- **Help others.** Voluntary work can really put your problems in perspective. There is usually a wonderful sense of camaraderie and the gratitude received more than outweighs the hours involved. Most charities are grateful for your input, from selling flags to sorting jumble. If you're feeling lonely, a stint at one of the charity shops will bring you into contact with the general public. Otherwise there are any number of options; meals-on-wheels, hospital visiting, riding for the disabled, reading to the blind, work with the old, young or handicapped. If you're looking forward to a miserable Christmas, then Crisis, who open their doors to the homeless for the winter holiday week, have a network of twenty-nine centres around the country, any one of which would be glad of a few hours of your time. And if you think your recent experience might make you more sympathetic to other abandonees, you could offer to man a phone at

Dignity, who run a nationwide telephone helpline for those suddenly at the end of their tether.

- **Get involved.** Choose a political party or cause dear to your heart and support it. This could be anything from Save the Whales to the local Citizens against Turning the Park into Parking Spaces Protest Group. Go to rallies and meetings. Make your voice heard. Don't think you can't make a difference. You *can*.
- **Learn.** Check out your local adult education college, or library. If there's a subject you've always been fascinated by, now's the time to pursue it. If you've got kids, don't let that deter you. Many courses have crèches attached. If yours doesn't, ask why not. Go to lectures, take classes, enrol on a course. Education broadens the mind.
- **Teach.** If you have a particular skill or talent, you might like to offer your services to any of the above. If your qualifications are more practical than academic, don't think you have nothing going for you. Put an ad in the local newsagent's saying you are starting a cake-baking (or curtain-making or poetry appreciation or abandoned women's self-help) group in your front room. Wisdom is without price and life experience much more valuable than diplomas.

We are all interconnected. When you are abandoned you tend to forget this. You feel isolated, deserted, alone.

Below is a list of headings. It represents your support system. Before you go on to the next chapter, take time to jot down the appropriate names beside each category. Some headings may not be relevant. Add extra headings if you need to. Don't leave anybody out. Do it *now*.

1. Friends.
2. Acquaintances.

3. Immediate family.
4. Extended family.
5. Work colleagues.
6. Cleaner/gardener/handyman.
7. Nanny/au pair/childminder/kid's teacher.
8. Doctor/dentist/optician.
9. Hairdresser/masseuse/exercise instructor.
10. Spiritual advisor (Your local vicar or anyone you have read who inspires you).
11. Therapist/counsellor.
12. Alternative therapist.
13. Milkman/postman/windowcleaner/ that nice cheerful person at the corner shop.
14. Role models (people whom you admire, in your own circle or in public life).

When you've finished, read the whole thing over. And you thought nobody cared!

Survival Strategy 7
Yoga

One of the good things about yoga is that it can be approached on many levels.

The physical exercises stretch and tone the body, massage the internal organs and promote deep relaxation. Known as *asana*, they are suitable for people of any age and virtually any state of health, though certain extreme postures are not recommended for people with a detached retina or a heart condition. It is best to begin to study under the tutelage of an experienced teacher but once the relevant positions have been mastered, along with the synchronized breathing which compliments them, then it is possible to practise alone. All one needs is a mat, a warm, quiet setting and twenty minutes or so of free time. Converts insist that those twenty minutes, regularly taken, can mean the difference between serenity and insanity.

The breathing techniques, known as *pranayama*, ensure that the student doesn't hold the breath (pushing up the blood pressure), and promote proper utilization of health-giving oxygen into the system. Since the body can subsist for months without food, days without water but only minutes without air, the importance of this aspect cannot be over-emphasized.

It is a yogic belief that foods which have been tampered with are stripped of *prana*, the life-force, and are nutritionally dead. Yogic dietary principles, which, simplified, recommend the consumption of whole-foods, a restriction on meat and dairy products and a complete ban on stimulants, help counteract many of the major medical problems such as bowel cancer, ulcers, allergies and cholesterol build-up that are now known to be directly linked to the overprocessed Western diet.

For enthusiasts who wish to progress to the more esoteric realms, transcendental meditation is said to still the mind, free the spirit, harness the autonomic system (the heart rate and blood pressure, not normally under control of the will) and help the subject become more at one with the universe.

Some masters of the yogic art have so far extended their control as to reach beyond themselves and their immediate environment and defy the logical laws of matter. Though levitation is unproven, it is an undisputed fact that some have been buried alive for days in that state of suspended animation peculiar to hibernation. Others defy pain by walking on burning coals, lying on beds of nails or sticking sharp objects through their flesh without apparent discomfort or even loss of blood.

Such control can only be obtained through years of study and devotion so don't, as they say, try this at home.

Yet yoga is not a religion. It neither recognizes nor excludes particular sects. It has been successfully integrated into the lives of people from diverse races, colours and creeds over many millennia. Its origins lie in India and can be traced, through cave paintings, at least as far back as 3,000 BC. Its many facets are perhaps best described in the *Bhagavad Gita*, the definitive treatise on the subject. In this poem, part of a much larger work known as the *Mahabharata*, the God Khrishna explains the philosophy and practice of yoga to the warrior Arjuna:

> Yoga is equilibrium in success and failure; yoga is skilful living among activities; yoga is the supreme secret of life; yoga is the producer of the greatest happiness; yoga

is effected by self-control; yoga is non-attachment; yoga
is the destroyer of pain; yoga is serenity.

There are many different strands of yoga – jhana, kharma, shakti, raja, mantra, hatha, tantric, khundulini and laya. They are all woven together to form a path to the same goal: spiritual enlightenment. They have as their starting point certain common basic rules of conduct. Ten commandments, positive in spirit. The first five, grouped under the heading *yama*, prohibit violence, stealing, covetousness, dishonesty and incontinence. The second five, *niyama*, encourage the observation of purity, austerity, contentment, study and devotion.

Most Western yoga classes will generally only incorporate two of the strands, hatha (dealing with the body) and raja (through the body to the mind). But even this 'lowest common denominator' approach is thought to be the first step to a better understanding of oneself and one's personal place in the grand design.

15 • Moving On

Until now I have recommended that after an abandonment you should stay put if possible. However, once you've got your head together, you may decide that relocating is a positive move. Or through force of circumstances or economic necessity, you may *have* to move. In either case, keep in mind that a house is not a home, it's just bricks and mortar.

It's possible to get so attached to a piece of property that it begins to own you rather than the other way round. This is especially true if you feel you have lost part of your identity with your man's defection. Many abandoned women talk of 'becoming invisible' when their men move on and in this instance what's left of your self-worth can become bound up with your living space. You secretly fear that in moving house you will cease to be.

Not so.

My former home in Aberdeen was an 1826 listed granite townhouse, built on three floors, with a garden, a double garage, a winecellar, moulded ceilings, wooden shutters, big walk-in cupboards and a twenty-four-foot kitchen that was to die for. I *loved* that house. It was like a security blanket.

But here's the strange thing. On the miserable November day that I moved out to travel south to a rented, unmodernized flat in London, it was borne in on me that what I was leaving was just four walls. As each piece of furniture, painting or book was removed, until nothing but the carpeting remained, the house became more and more of a husk, less and less of a sanctuary. And I realized, with thankful relief, that it wasn't the house, but what we'd brought to it, that had made it so special. The spirit that had conjured life into the wood and stone would travel with us to our next location. My son and I could be happy elsewhere. Anywhere, in fact.

You never truly own anything. I had custody of that wonderful house for twelve years, I nurtured and cherished it and I will always remember it fondly. But I don't regret leaving it, even though I moved to a flat a quarter of the size that didn't even have a washing-machine. It had got to the point when I could no longer afford the upkeep of the place. I was doing everybody a favour in letting it go to a nice young couple who would inject a little cash into it and fill it with parties and babies and cherish it just as much as I had.

If you've reached the time when you feel you have to move on, take a few moments to assess what you lose and what you gain by your decision. That way you'll be prepared for any stumbling blocks.

Some Points Against Moving

1. Moving is a serious life upheaval. It's also hard work. You think you don't own anything until you try to pack it.

2. Radical change which cuts to the heart of your security is bound to raise your stress levels. Are you ready for it?

3. If you move to a smaller house or flat (almost inevitable if you are going because of economic necessity), you may find that much of your furniture doesn't fit and you have to jettison some of your favourite pieces. Are you willing to let them go with no regrets?

4. If you move out of the area, you will be losing valuable

support systems. Not only friends but also your familiar doctor, dentist, schools. This is what happens when older people retire and move away. It may be a dream they have cherished all their lives but what they leave behind is much more precious: familiar routines, good friendships, a lifetime's memories. Sometimes they never settle and, if one of them dies, the other can become very lonely.

5. If you have kids, all of the above also applies to them. They will have to cope with the same stress, loss of friends and a drop in living standards, and they don't have any control over the situation. Children are notoriously resilient, but if they're already unsettled, the move to a new environment can be traumatic. You will have to be there for them body and soul until they settle down. Are you strong enough for that? In taking them out of school try to make it coincide with a natural break (between primary and secondary education, for instance) or at least the end of the school year. Otherwise their school work, their self-esteem and their security will suffer in equal measure. If force of circumstance means you can't line up the house sale with one of these milestones, consider boarding them with friends for a couple of weeks rather than moving them mid-term.

6. If you move away, the children will lose access to their father (assuming that he's still around).

7. If there's negative equity involved, obviously it's better to try to hang on until the market improves.

Some Points in Favour of Moving

1. It can be an exciting new start, opening up fresh possibilities, which might never have occurred to you in

your old environment – anything from retraining to overseas work.

2. It's a clean break from the past, laying to rest memories of happier times. And, since no one will know your ex where you're going, you'll be accepted as a person in your own right rather than as the deserted half of a couple.

3. It can be a great relief if your ex is living round the corner with his new partner. No chance of bumping into them in the street, something which can put your recovery back by months.

4. Less access for the children to their father is a bonus if he's violent, alcoholic, or unstable (liable to kidnap the kids – or threaten to do so).

5. If there's positive equity, you can realize your assets. With luck this will give you enough money for a down payment on something smaller and leave some sort of nest egg to tide you over while you decide what to do next. However, bear in mind that it is *very* expensive to move house. With estate agents' and solicitors' fees at both ends and the exorbitant charges of removal firms, you could be looking at £6,000 off your profit just to get from A to B.

If you choose to move, it is vital to reinvest your money immediately or it will just dribble away. Remember though, that if you are a single woman with a low-paid job or no visible means of support, you will find it very difficult to get another mortgage. This goes double if you are over forty. Before you sell, see whether the manager of your current building society or bank will recommend you to another branch as a reliable prospect. If you have an accountant, ask his advice.

What to Do if You Have to Move

- Get your name on the local authority housing list straight away.

- Double up. If you are staying in the same area and have a friend in similar circumstances, you might consider sharing accommodation. It's not true that two can live as cheaply as one but two can certainly live cheaper together than apart. In a rented house, where you can have a floor each and share a kitchen and bathroom, you'd only be paying half of all the standing charges on utilities, plus half the rates. Unless you are both single with no children, sharing a flat is probably not an option. There's simply not enough personal space.

- Take a live-in job. For instance, as a housekeeper or companion. This is a particularly good option for someone older who feels they are unqualified but who has been successfully running a home for years.

- Try not to move in with your mother (or daughter): it rarely works.

At one point I thought of starting a housing association for abandoned women. Women of a certain age, pooling their resources, could live in more salubrious circumstances than a single female struggling on alone. Since each would have their own flat in a larger property, they would also be a source of mutual social support.

The Practicalities of Moving

Having found a new place to live and sold the old one, here's what you do:

1. Get rid of everything you don't want, need or are

unlikely to use again. Do this *before* you move.

Work out what you can leave behind and use it to bump up the asking price. Kitchen appliances, obviously. Fixtures and fittings: carpets (a bind to lift and they won't fit at your new place), curtains, blinds, light-fittings (probably won't match the décor).

Have a garage sale or make use of the small ads section of your local paper. You can normally advertise items worth up to a certain amount (usually £50.00) free. Alternatively, look in the *Yellow Pages* for companies that do house clearances and get a quote. Don't be offended if it's low. Second-hand furniture fetches nothing and the guys have to make a profit. Be prepared to haggle.

Anything you can't sell – give away. Bequeath large plants to plant-loving friends or the local hospital. Small plants don't travel well either. Take cuttings and start afresh at your next destination. Anything too shabby for the charity shops should be left out for the bin-men. Someone may take it away before they arrive.

Be prepared to spend a good month on the clear out. If you're a hoarder, you may need the help of a good friend to stiffen your resolve. You'll feel as light as a feather when it's done. The more you clear away the more space you leave for better things.

If you have children, let them do their own sorting. Don't throw anything away without telling them. They'll never forgive you. And rightly so.

2. Get three quotes from reputable removal companies. Don't necessarily choose the cheapest. Each will send a representative round to assess the amount of furniture and any special packing needs. Be prepared for eloquent speeches and glossy brochures. Take both with a pinch of salt. Read the small print before you sign the

contract. You'll be horrified to discover how heavily weighted it is in the company's favour and what little compensation you are entitled to whatever they do to the antique furniture. Make sure you keep all the paperwork. And if you do have to claim, you must put it in writing within ten days or you forfeit your recompensatory rights.

3. If you can afford it, pay the extra to have the company do the packing (and unpacking). Then go out while they do it. The insurance doesn't apply unless they do so (if *you* pack and your best china gets broken, you have no come-back because you can't prove it wasn't packed that way). The drawback is that if they don't send enough men to unpack your stuff in the allocated time, you either have to unpack the rest of it yourself and risk that nothing has been broken, or make an appointment for them to come back to finish the job and live in a maze of packing cases for another ten days. Note that none of this is the fault of the men on the ground, who will still expect a sizeable tip!

4. Don't forget to have the gas and electricity men come and take a final reading on the meters and ask the phone company to bill you before you move out. Arrange for the people into whose property you are moving to do the same. Provided they are leaving the kitchen fittings behind, this saves the trouble (and expense) of having the utilities reconnected. More importantly, you can plug in the kettle and make a cup of tea as soon as you arrive.

5. If you make a reasonable profit, put your belongings in store and go off for a holiday for a couple of weeks on the day you move out. Somewhere sunny, where you can lie down a lot. Arrange to have the furniture

delivered to your new address on the day you come back. Storage is surprisingly cheap and, since you'll arrive rested and refreshed, it minimizes the overload of packing and unpacking on the same day. Which is a killer.

16 • Moving In

When the removal men finally left my new premises I stood in the middle of the living room and cried. You try fitting the contents of a three-storey house into a two-bedroom flat. Even after all the furniture had been distributed, the curtains hung, the linen and clothes squirrelled away, I still had twenty-five packing cases of miscellaneous stuff stashed in the hall.

How to Fit a Quart into a Pint Pot

1. Be creative. I have a cabin trunk, which used to be kept in the attic but which now doubles as coffee table in the lounge and holds my summer clothes. Come April I replace these with my winter clothes. I also use the change around to get rid of anything that's gone out of fashion in the interim.

2. Adapt. We have a dustbin cupboard in the hall outside the flat which holds ladders, fold down beds, wellies and everything *except* the dustbin. Check whether you have a similar space you could utilize (corner of a garage, old potting shed) to leave more living space free.

3. Put things on top of other things. Wardrobes can support plastic stacking boxes or laundry hampers which are great for holding handbags or shoes or winter weight duvets (in the summertime) or all those old photographs

that you intend to put in albums one of these days.

4. If you have one child and two bunk beds take the bottom bunk out and use the space underneath for a sofa, desk, hanging space.

5. Put things underneath things. Store things under beds. Or under tables which you don't use much. Cover them with a colourful throw or a heavy plush tablecloth for camouflage.

6. Put things behind things. A sofa, pulled a foot away from the wall, will conceal a set of suitcases.

7. Put things inside things. Fill the suitcases with winter clothes or whatever. Unless you're very lucky, you only use suitcases once or twice a year. When you're off on holiday dump the contents on the bedroom floor until you get back. You're not going to have to look at it while you're away. Or stack suitcases inside each other, like Russian dolls. Small items can be stored in make-up bags or handbags that you only use once in a blue moon.

8. Be original. Who says the filing cabinet can't go in the bedroom? If there's room there and nowhere else, why not?

9. Hang stuff on walls. God bless the person who invented shelves. Kitchen units can be placed above work-surfaces, bookshelves in the hall, CD and tapes above the sound system. If you don't have much cupboard space, collapsible wicker shelf units are light enough to go on top of other units, like the sideboard, or free-stand on top of each other in the kitchen to keep storage jars, crockery and saucepans neat and tidy. And wicker cutlery drawers can be stacked one on top of another and used to store make-up, first aid, do-it-yourself kit, cleaning equipment, bathroom toiletries.

Incidentally, if you are taking a cut in living standards don't assume you are hard done by just because everybody else has something you don't. Ask yourself. Do you really need it? As I mentioned before, the flat I moved into has no washing machine. But there's a good side to everything. For a fiver a week the local launderette does a service wash. This frees me up to do something more constructive (like write this book). It also saves energy and running costs which can be substantial. My laundry comes back neatly folded and ready to be put away. Smalls, hand-washed of an evening and hung over the bath, are dry by next morning. If had a baby or several small children, doing without a washing machine would be a challenge I wouldn't like to have to face, but in my situation I've never truly missed it.

If you've left a beautiful house and are feeling down and deprived, remind yourself that this is merely a temporary situation. Things can only get better. Meanwhile take Theodore Roosevelt's advice and 'Do the best you can with what you've got where you are.'

Survival Strategy 8
Sanctuary

A sanctuary is a place where you are safe: a sacred space where no enemy can enter nor any harm befall you.

Your home should be a sanctuary. A haven of peace. A hedge against the world in times of trouble. Unfortunately, more often than not, home is a battleground in which people do cruel and hurtful things to each other in the name of love. For some of us, brought up in dysfunctional households, the concept of home as a sanctuary is a difficult, if not impossible, one to grasp. Why do you think so many men stay out at the pub? Or women, left behind, come to view their homes more as a prison than retreat?

If this has been your experience, now's the time to change it. It makes no difference if you live in a castle or a council flat; you can transform your living space into a sanctuary. Here's your chance to make it into an area of warmth and comfort designed for rejuvenation and regrowth.

Let's begin with the five senses. Too often nowadays the senses are poisoned by artificial stimulants or dulled by information overload. Our aim is to utilize each of them in the creation of an enabling environment.

Sight

- Candles create a soft and soothing atmosphere and come in all shapes and sizes, from tiny nightlights to giant pillars of beeswax. Fat and stubby, tall and elegant, round, square and oblong, you can buy them at specialist shops or in craft fairs or markets. Some are scented, others shaped like apples or pine-cones or sunflowers or stars. You can match them to the colour of your décor, display them in novelty holders cut out to produce soft patterns of light, or float them in crystal bowls like chinese water-lanterns. They are a delight to the eye. Dot them round the room in groups. Make them into a shrine alongside flowers and fruit. Allow them to sparkle off a special piece of crystal or glass. If you have a new beau to dine, candles on the table reflect in the eyes and are exceptionally kind to the complexion. (Of course any naked flame can be a fire hazard, so if you have children best keep your candles in a private place like your bedroom.)

- Colours can influence our moods so choose your colours with care. Sunny yellow for a good morning kitchen, blues or lilacs for a tranquil sleeping area, green for a nurturing feeling, earth tones for warmth. Transform a gloomy flat by painting it white all through and adding a few large green plants for a Spanish villa effect.

- Flowers, plants, herbs. The first and last of these provide both visual and olfactory stimulation. All three encourage nurturing qualities. You have to tend plants. So if you're feeling alone and unloved, pour your affection into them and watch them flourish. And, yes, do talk to them. Plants thrive on sunlight and oxygen and water. Breathing on them while you chat during their daily spraying really will nourish them, and make you feel better too.

- Pictures and photos remind you of happy times, good friends. Have some in every room. Buy a cheap cork noticeboard and make a collage or just stick them up with drawing pins if you can't afford frames.

- Mirrors bring light and brightness into a house. Pick them up at auctions or in charity shops. Set flowers and plants in front of them to double the effect. A couple of dozen daffodils can look like Wordsworth's golden host displayed this way. Place mirrors next to windows to maximize sunlight. Use them to reflect candles or lamplight and bring warmth to a dull room.

- Be creative with lighting. Use pockets of it to emphasize special features like a piece of pottery, a reading corner. Pink bulbs in the bedroom or by your make-up mirror will soften the effect if you look more raddled than ravishing. Relegate harsh strip lights to areas like kitchen worksurfaces. Use angle-poise lamps in the office or study.

- Crystals can be very pretty and are an excellent aid to meditation. Put them on the window-sill in summer, to absorb the sunlight. Then place them at the four corners while you're in the bath. And a collection of stones picked up from various beaches, placed in a glass jar filled with water (to intensify the colours and striations), will humidify a room and make a cheap and decorative bookend.

- Shells. More treasure trove from the beach. Or you can now buy some glorious specimens from specialist shops. A single conch shell is as delicate as a rose and longer lasting. Smaller shells, heaped in a wicker basket in the bathroom, are a relaxing reminder of warm sunny beaches or brisk winter walks by the sea.

- Buy a mat with 'welcome' on it and put it right inside the front door. Every time you come back exhausted from the supermarket or a hard day at the office, you'll see it and feel glad to be home.

Sound

Anyone coming from the past would find the twentieth century incredibly noisy. We are assailed by traffic, low-flying aircraft and techno played at 500 decibels above the pain threshold. This is sound as irritant.

Children nowadays do their homework with headsets and the television on. Some houses are never silent. Ask your teenager to turn off his tranny and he'll look at you as though you've taken leave of your senses. This is sound as company.

It's as if somehow we've grown afraid of silence. As though in the quiet moment, we'll find out something about ourselves that we'd rather not know.

- Silence is golden. Treat yourself to some peace and quiet. Try turning everything off and just tuning in to the sound of your own breathing, your soft footfalls on the carpet, the birds singing outside.

- Wind-chimes have an ethereal quality. Hang a set at the front door so that every time you open it, the hall is filled with music.

- White sound. Waves, bird-song, sounds of the forest, whale music. Fill your home with the relaxing sounds of nature. My favourite piece is called *Ocean Waves at Sunset*. Whatever state I'm in, it's guaranteed to calm me down. The sound of waves is similar to the first sounds we hear in the womb, so it's also good for soothing a fractious toddler at nap-time.

- Easy listening. Not musak, but something that relaxes you. Gregorian chants are good. Pan pipes. Or anything that reminds you of good times. My brother Michael bought me a tape of KD lang on a recent trip to New Zealand (where he lives). I heard it first while we were having Sunday lunch at a beautiful Winery in Hawkes Bay called

The Mission. Every time I play it I remember that wonderful lunch, and the late December sunshine streaming through the windows of that lovely dining room on the other side of the world.

PS. Noël Coward wrote that you should 'never underestimate the potency of cheap music', so best to put 'your song' on the bottom of the pile for the duration.

- A pet bird. Budgies chatter but finches and canaries sing. As I write, my black-headed zebra finch Max is hanging in the window singing his heart out. I carry him with me from room to room so that he can have a change of scene and we chat intermittently through the day.

Smell

Smell is probably the most evocative sense of all. Coffee and brandy actually smell better than they taste. One whiff of a Gauloise, and I'm back in the arms of a French jazz guitarist with whom I had a short-lived but passionate affair in the seventies. Here are some ways to scent your sanctuary:

- Aromatic oil burners. Made of pottery, the heat from the nightlight rises to vaporize the oil and fills the room with fragrance – anything from vanilla to pine. The Body Shop sells them or you can pick them up at craft fairs.

- Joss sticks. Pungent smells of the East. Very 1960s. From Indian shops or Oxfam.

- Pot pourri. Dot around the house in your favourite pottery bowls.

- Smelly plugs. You can now buy scented three-pin electric plugs which emit a delicious pong of summer haze or spring flowers or whatever. Refills available.

- Lavender sachets. Put them in your wardrobe and drawers

to make your smalls smell sensational. Make them yourself if you've got time on your hands and a lavender bush in your garden. They make great Christmas and birthday presents.

Don't use chemical perfume room sprays if you value the ozone layer.

Taste

The twentieth-century lifestyle has us eating on the hoof, shovelling food into ourselves so fast that, as Tony Hancock said (of Hattie Jaques and a plate of macaroni cheese), it 'hardly has time to touch the sides on the way down'.

- Try to savour your food, rather than wolfing it as though there were no tomorrow.

- Don't watch TV while you're eating. This goes double for the news. If there's something unpleasant on, you'll ingest the bad vibes along with the food and give yourself indigestion.

- If you have kids at home, set a proper table. And try to make the meal an enjoyable experience for them rather than an excuse to continually correct their manners or urge them to eat up. Don't take it as a personal insult if they refuse the food you've so lovingly prepared. It's not rejection – they're probably just not hungry. Check their in-between snack intake and don't have sweets, crisps and digestive biscuits in the house (for your sake as well as theirs). Apples are better for their teeth.

- Think of the way the Italians eat. Food as entertainment. Three-hour meals with pauses between courses for digestion and communication. I know this isn't practical if you have a schedule to stick to, but what about Sundays?

Sanctuary

- Invite friends to share Sunday lunch. A plate of spaghetti and a bottle of plonk won't cost a fortune, fills the house with warmth and laughter and keeps your nurturing skills in good shape. If you invite five people, it should also open you up to five dinner invitations sometime in the near future. (As long as you don't spend the whole time moaning about 'that man'.)

- Don't eat and run (or *on* the run). Better to rise half an hour earlier and have a leisurely breakfast than be stuffing croissants down your gullet halfway down the drive.

- Buy the best your budget will stand. A good cider is better than a bad wine, a superb sausage preferable to a tough steak.

- Retrain the palate away from endless cups of tea and de-caffeinated sludge to cool water, fresh juice, herb teas.

- Treat the taste-buds to real food rather than irradiated rubbish. Think succulent fruits, crisp stir-fried vegetable, salads dressed in virgin olive oil, wine vinegar, fresh ground black pepper and pure sea-salt. New-laid eggs with buttered soldiers, fresh herrings rolled in oatmeal, warm bread with chunks of cheese.

- At weekends breakfast in bed the French way. Hot croissants with apricot jam, big bowls of steaming coffee and, if you're on your own, the Sunday papers. Utter bliss. And a much healthier way to start the day than greasy bacon and eggs.

- Plump for quality not quantity. A small jar of caviar, some pumpernickel and a glass of dry white wine won't cost any more than an oven-ready meal or a take-away pizza.

- Be adventurous. Add diversity to your diet with some ethnic cooking: Indian, Chinese, Greek, Italian, Mexican.

- Herbs and spices add a sensory sub-plot to otherwise plain ingredients. Cloves in mulled wine. Spiced peaches with ham. Dill and coriander, nutmeg and ginger. Fresh if you can get them. Grow parsley and chives on your window-sill. Start a herb garden. Plant a chamomile lawn.

Incidentally, if you smoke, your sense of smell and taste will both be impaired. Two out of five. Think of what you're missing. Another good reason to give it up . . .

Touch

Touch is a way to open the love channels so that they don't heal up. In the section on massage I said we touch too little these days. I want to say it again. Touch is healing, comforting, nurturing. There's something seriously amiss with a society that makes a grandfather hesitate before hugging a beloved granddaughter for fear someone might mistake him for a dirty old man. Touch will put you back *in* touch if you are feeling alienated and alone.

- Pets. A great source of comfort. Dogs will love you even first thing in the morning without your make-up on, while stroking a cat is therapeutic for both you and the cat. And on the aural front is there anything more relaxing than the sound of a cat's purr? Even something small like a gerbil needs tending and is a source of amusement, not to mention company. And, in taking care of them, there's less chance that you will let yourself go.

- Children. Cuddles are as comforting for you as for them. Instead of plonking them in front of the TV, sit them on your knee and read to them. The dishes can wait. And a massage will still a crying baby better than a dummy.

- Friends. Be tactile. Lots of hugs. A pat on the shoulder. A squeeze of the arm. Touch is the ultimate communication. Invite people into your personal space.

- Warm water. Bliss for tired feet. Soak them in a basinful while watching the telly. And there's still nothing to beat a warm bath for soothing aching muscles and sluicing away the cares of the day (see below).
- Wherever possible use sensual fabrics for tactile pleasure. Silk next to the skin. Velvet cushions. Satin sheets. Mohair rugs. Warm winter woollies.

The Bath Ritual

Even if you normally take showers, at least once a week allow yourself the luxury of a wallow in a long hot bath. Set aside an hour. Late Sunday morning (after your breakfast and the papers) is a good time if you're alone. Any evening after the kids are safely tucked up in bed if you're not. Play soothing music or wave sounds. If you have them, place your crystals at the four corners. If it's evening, turn off the main lights in favour of candles. Place them in front of a mirror for extra effect. Take off any old nail varnish, remove all your make-up, tie back your hair, slap on a face pack, place some soothing teabags or cool slices of cucumber over your eyes and relax for at least twenty minutes. Better than a week's holiday.

Bedtime Bonus

Instead of getting into bed full of jitters and thrashing around for hours in insomniac hell, prepare for the experience as you would for a special treat. The run-down will put you in sleep mode and help you nod off with no trouble. Make a hot-water bottle. Fix a warm drink: Horlicks or hot milk or chamomile tea. Read (romance rather than horror) and relax. If you're feeling tense, play a relaxation tape to soothe you. Focus on the good things that have happened during the day. Anticipate the better things that are going to occur tomorrow. If you have a current problem (or challenge!), don't worry about it. Instead offer it up to your subconscious and let it go. A solution will probably present itself by the morning. *Don't* watch TV – especially late-night thrillers. Much too stimulating. And avoid vigorous exercise, though a stroll round the block with the dog won't do you any harm, provided you live in a safe area. Sweet dreams.

A Sanctuary Filled with Books

Books evoke all five senses at once through the power of your imagination; they are magic of the most potent sort. They can alter your reality. Humorous books can make you laugh when you're feeling down. Others can transport you into different dimensions or foreign territories. Books transcend time and space. They can transform your bedroom into a futuristic space ship or a haunted historical castle. Uplifting books can mean the beginning of a beautiful friendship – with yourself. They can improve your perspective, open up your world, change your life. Invest in knowledge. Get books from the library, from second-hand stores, from charity shops, from book-clubs. Books are always there for you and old favourites stand reading again and again. They can turn your home into an oasis of learning.

None of the above should be thought of as self-indulgence. In cherishing yourself you are conveying a strong message to your subconscious that you are worthy of all the good things the universe has to offer. Cherishing yourself makes it easier to accept cherishing from other people, which can be difficult if you've been badly betrayed and feel you may never trust anyone again.

It's love, not sex, that makes the world go round. Take time to make your home a loving place and you need never feel deprived again.

17 • DIY for Idiots

Rule one (about doing it yourself): wherever possible get someone else to show you how . . .

If you buy a piece of equipment check whether it has a battery – or whatever it needs to make it function – before you leave the shop. If it hasn't, ask the nice sales assistant to do the needful.

To retain control over your life, however, you need to learn to cope with the rudiments of home maintenance on your own. Forget early conditioning. There is nothing unladylike about being self-sufficient. Contrary to common supposition, you don't have to be built like an all-in wrestler to change a car wheel.

Rule two: if a job's worth doing, it's worth doing right, and it's impossible to do it right without the proper tools. Just as you wouldn't apply your eye make-up with a trowel, so you shouldn't attempt to mend a fuse armed with a nail-file.

Here is a list of basics which you should have in the house against the evil day. With luck your ex may have left some items behind. Check before you buy. If the list seems somewhat formidable, remind yourself that it is an investment – one which will pay for itself the very next time you don't have to call the plumber out to change a washer. Get everything you can from a hardware store where you can ask for advice.

This is what you'll need for openers:

DIY for Idiots

1. A well-illustrated DIY manual.
2. A retractable tape-measure (for judging the length of a piece of string).
3. A piece of string. A couple of balls in fact, one thick, for clotheslines and such, one thinner, for odds and ends.
4. A hammer (with a prong at one side for pulling out nails).
5. A pair of pliers (for stripping wires).
6. A good, strong collapsible ladder (you can get ones that double as a kitchen stool) for replacing light bulbs.
7. A set of screwdrivers (with insulated handles for electrical work).
8. Several spare plugs.
9. A large tube of clear, all-purpose glue. (You can add other more specific fixatives as and when you need them).
10. A Stanley knife and a couple of pairs of scissors (one strong and sturdy, one smaller – for fiddly bits).
11. A box of 3-amp and 13-amp fuses and a couple of packets of fuse-wire.
12. Nails, screws, tacks, picture-hooks, curtain hooks. (Although you're almost certain to find tins of these hanging around somewhere.)
13. A rubber plunger (the large size) for unblocking drains.
14. An adjustable spanner.
15. Candles for power cuts. A torch (with batteries) for finding candles during the power cuts. A large box of matches (to save you hunting for the kitchen ones in

the dark), to light the candles when you've found them.

If you don't already have one, it's a good idea to have a basic First Aid kit (Savlon, bandages, safety pins, Elastoplast and TCP) in case you cut yourself with the Stanley knife, skin your knee tripping over the flex you shouldn't have left lying around, or drop the hammer on your toe.

When you get home, put all your equipment away in one place — a drawer in the kitchen or, even better, in one of those plastic cutlery trays which have separate compartments to make sure the screws stay out of the glues. Congratulations. Having the correct tools to hand is the first step to being a successful maintenance person, and, with your basic toolbox sorted out, you've cleared the biggest psychological hurdle that faces women when they think about do-it-yourself. You've said, 'I can do that.'

How to Fit a Plug

Consumer legislation has changed recently so all new appliances now have to be sold with a plug attached. However, most appliances have obsolescence built in (otherwise we'd never need to buy another iron and then where would the consumer society be?). Before you throw your heated rollers in the bin and spend money on another set, try changing the plug.

1. Unscrew the old plug with a small screwdriver.
2. Set the top aside.
3. In the bottom you will find a fuse — small cylindrical object. This can be slipped out and replaced quite easily. Often this is what has gone wrong so replace it, screw the top back on and try the hair rollers or

whatever again. If they work, you need read no further; if not . . .

4. Cut off the old plug and discard it. Find a new plug. Unscrew it as before. There should be a little coloured diagram attached to it showing how to wire it. If so, just follow those instructions. If there isn't . . .

5. Strip the outer flex back an inch and a half to disclose the three coloured wires.

6. Thread the outer flex through the hole at the base of the plug so that the coloured wires are inside.

7. Place the wires adjacent to their relevant terminals: looking down on them with the flex hole nearest your body, they should lie blue (neutral) to the left, stripey green and yellow (earth) top centre and brown (live) on the right.

8. Using your Stanley knife, cut the coloured plastic back to expose the copper wires underneath.

9. Thread the wires through their appropriate terminals and screw in tight, making sure that they lie flat against the bottom of the plug; they are quite secure; and no copper or coloured bits protrude from the flex hole when you've screwed the top and bottom together again.

10. Screw the top and bottom together again.

11. Give the flex a light tug to make sure nothing's going to come apart.

12. Switch off the wall socket. Plug in the plug. Switch on the wall socket. Switch on the appliance.

How to Unblock a Sink

Never throw old cooking fat down the sink. It may be hot when you pour it away but it will solidify when it hits the cold water in the U bend. Instead, pour it into a screw-top jar, leave it to harden and chuck the whole caboodle in the bin.

Whatever the cause, you can unblock a sink from two directions.

Stage 1: from the top
1. Buy some soda crystals from the supermarket.
2. Pour a cupful down the sink.
3. Follow that with half a cup of salt and half a cup of biological washing powder.
4. Pour down a couple of kettles of boiling water.

With a bit of luck that should clear it. If it doesn't, go on to . . .

Stage 2: still from the top
5. Get the plunger from under the sink.
6. Push a damp dishcloth into the overflow outlet to create a vacuum. NB Don't use kitchen paper, it will just dissolve and make matters worse.
7. Fit the working end of the plunger over the sink hole and pump vigorously. Imagine your sink can't breathe and you are giving it artificial respiration. If you are successful, you will be rewarded by a gurgling sound as the sink comes round. If not, it's time to move on to . . .

Stage 3: from the bottom
8. Put a bucket under the U bend.

9. Put on pair of rubber gloves.
10. Remove the big screw/screws at the bottom of the U bend. You'll need a wrench for this.
11. Whatever's blocking the sink should slop or slither out like something from a horror movie. If it doesn't, poke a skewer up to loosen it.
12. Replace the screw. Tightly. Run some water before you take the bucket away to make sure it's tight enough.
13. Discard the gloop.
14. Repeat instructions 2, 3 and 4.

How to Change a Washer

There is nothing quite as irritating as a dripping tap. No wonder the Chinese used it as a form of torture. It also wastes an amazing amount of water (and money, if you're on a meter) and bumps up your heating bill (if it's the hot tap). Dripping is usually caused by a worn-out washer and won't stop until you replace it. Here's how. Call a plumber and get them to show you how to do it. Pay attention so that you never have to do so again.

How to Change a Tyre

It's not so long ago that, if you had a blow-out and were struggling to change a wheel by the side of the road, you could confidently expect some kind bloke to stop and assist. Nowadays, unless absolutely necessary, don't. If you regularly make long journeys by car, then it's sensible to invest in a mobile phone. (I know I said earlier on that these were an unnecessary expense, but this is the exception.) Then if a tyre goes, get the vehicle off the road, call the AA or RAC and wait, inside, with the doors locked, until they come and rescue you. If you're not a member of the AA or RAC, call the police. They should be able to put you in touch with the nearest garage who will send someone out.

At home, of course, it's a different matter. If you're a member of the AA or RAC, check first whether you have a home-start facility, in which case call them. No point in doing anything you don't *have* to. If you haven't or you're in a tearing hurry and there's an hour and a half delay, here's what to do:

1. Make sure the handbrake is on and the car is in gear. If the car is on a slope put a brick under the downhill wheel for extra safety.

2. Find your spare wheel and your car tool-kit (which should have a jack in it). Unload them on to the pavement.

3. Unscrew hub-cap (if you have one).

4. Loosen the wheel-nuts with a spanner but don't remove them yet.

5. Jack up the car (check your handbook for correct positioning) until the wheel is well off the ground.

6. Take the wheel-nuts off and put them inside the car on the dashboard, so they don't roll off down the road never to be seen again.

7. Take off the wheel.

8. Fit on the spare wheel.

9. Put the nuts back on and tighten them.

10. Lower the car until the wheel touches the ground.

11. Re-tighten the nuts.

DIY for Idiots

12. Remove the jack.
13. Put back the hub-cap (if you have one).
14. Pack everything away (except the spanner).
15. As a final precaution, drive to the nearest garage, check the tyre pressure and re-tighten the nuts one last time.

While you're there, leave the punctured wheel to be repaired. If you don't do it straight away, you'll forget and then the next time you get a puncture, you *will* be in trouble.

General Car Maintenance

Most of us hardly pay any attention to our car until something goes wrong. Yet, as with human bodies, a little tender loving care can go a long way. Set aside a regular time for some basic maintenance. For what it's worth, three p.m. on a Tuesday seems to be the optimum time to beat the queues at the car wash and the air machine.

Weekly
- Check water.
- Refill windscreen washers.
- Check tyre pressure.
- Wash. Going to a car wash saves time and shouldn't cost more than a couple of quid, or let the kids do it by hand to earn their pocket money.

Monthly
- Check oil and top-up if necessary.
- Wax, again at the car wash (one price up) or by hand.

Every three months
- Touch up any rust spots with acrylic paint. (Buy it at your local accessory shop or garage.)

NB Come October, don't forget the anti-freeze!

18 • Goal-Setting

So you've got your head together, you're feeling better about yourself and your future. Now what? Where do you go from here?

Let's play a game. It's called goal-setting.

If I were minister for education, goal-setting would be a basic requirement of the national curriculum. Most people bumble through life with no idea of what they want or where they're going. Goal-setting is a way of getting things clear in your head. A map. A plan. A life skill. Much more relevant to a confused fifteen-year-old than economics or geography. And much more fun.

So. Get a piece of paper, or your journal. Take ten minutes to brainstorm. Write down all the things you would like to do, be or have. Not just what you want to own. What kind of a job you would like, where you want to live. Travel. Resources. Education. Treats. Don't analyse. Let your imagination run riot. Write continuously. Anything that pops into your head. There are no limits here. It doesn't matter whether what you aspire to seems impossible viewed from your present circumstances. Let your subconscious do the work. Dream. Putting those dreams on paper is a way of formalizing them. It's their first step into the real world. There's an old saying, 'What the mind can conceive, the mind can achieve.' This is the moment of conception.

Finished? Good.

Now take five minutes to review what you've written.

If you've spent the last twenty years of your life putting other people first, or if you have an underlying belief that wanting something for yourself is selfish, you may have a woefully short list. Don't worry about it. Goal-setting is a way of opening up your imagination to the unlimited possibilities of which you are the source. It gets easier with practice. If it is a short list, that is a lesson in itself. It means you need to do a bit more work on your self-esteem.

If you've got a list as long as your arm and you still have a couple of things you'd like to tack on, congratulations. You're beginning to get the hang of this self-approval lark.

Either way, take another five minutes to add some fine tuning.

Nothing more to add? Sure?

Now, take another piece of paper and divide your overall goals into three sections: *do*, *be* and *have*.

The *do* list should contain all the goals from your big list like travelling, studying, swimming well or reading the complete works of Ovid in the original Latin.

The *be* list is where you put career, educational and growth goals. Perhaps you want to be self-employed or take a degree or follow a particular spiritual path or just lose a little weight?

The *have* list is the fun one. Here you can put all the things you've always wanted to own: house, car, yacht, Armani jacket. Look back at your creative visualization lists if you run out of ideas.

Be specific. It's not enough to say that you want to be rich and famous. You need to quantify it: 'I want to be a successful corporate lawyer making £50,000 a year'. Forget about how. For the moment it is enough just to open your mind up to what.

Add a time-frame. If one of your *be* goals involves being in better shape then say, 'I will lose 7 lbs by next November.'

If your *do* list includes 'read more', say one book per week or whatever.

Embroider. Instead of just saying you want to hear Pavarotti sing, elaborate: 'I want to hear Pavarotti sing *La Bohème* in an open-air amphitheatre on a warm Tuscan night. And have a pizza afterwards!' Focus and have fun with it.

Weed out. While you're transferring things, consider each item briefly and make sure you really *do* want it. Eliminate anything half-hearted. Some things you'll think, 'No, that's not really important . . . it was just an idea.' If you feel that way, scrub it off the list. No point in confusing the issue with unnecessary clutter.

Prioritize. Pick the most important item from each list and, taking yet another piece of paper, divide each into mini-goals. For instance, for weight loss you could put:

1. Throw out all fattening goods.
2. Go to supermarket and do a healthy shop.
3. Join exercise class.
4. Lose 2 lbs this week.
5. Lose 7 lbs by the end of the month.

Now do something to start the ball rolling. Make a little chart with your statement of intent on it: 'I intend to lose 7 lbs by 1 November.' Then put today's date and beside it your weight and measurements. This should give you the impetus to go to the cupboard and get rid of all the junk food. Don't eat it on the premise that you're going on a diet tomorrow! Go off to the supermarket and get the healthy stuff and start *today*!

Each positive action reinforces your resolve. Each mini-goal achieved reinforces your feeling of success and self-worth. Pretty soon you'll have realized what was only an intention. And it began by your getting clear what it was that you wanted.

Do this with each list.

Now write one more list with your main goals from each of the three headings: what you would like to *be* (a successful writer); *do* (visit Machu Picchu); and *have* (a house in the sun).

You may find that your goals change over a period of time, that things which seemed important to you lose their appeal as other things move in to replace them. That's fine. Nothing is written in stone.

One last thing. That show-business phenomenon, the overnight success, when viewed up close, usually involves years of hard slog, learning the trade in back-street clubs or shifting scenery in and out of town theatres. Overnight successes who are manufactured by manipulative managers or unscrupulous record companies are generally the one-hit wonders who fade as fast as they appear or, worse, who find fame impossible to handle and fall by the wayside in a welter of sex, drugs and rock and roll.

We all have to pay our dues. Real, lasting success comes from doing a little every day. Rejoicing in small triumphs, dealing with minor set-backs. Day after day. So be sure that what you put on those lists is something you won't get tired of, something you're really interested in. Something that inspires you.

That inspiration will carry you through to achieve your goal. If it doesn't, you really didn't want it anyway.

Goal-setting is a practical way to clarify what you really want, at any given time, at any stage of your development. Use goal-setting to clear away confusion and establish your priorities.

Six months from now, look at the list you've written

today. You probably won't have achieved everything on it, but you'll be amazed at just how many things you have accomplished.

Some time ago. I did a goal-setting exercise at one of Tony Robbins' 'Date with Destiny' seminars. Among the many things on my list were a face-lift, a round-the-world trip, a move back to London and the opportunity to meet dishy blond filmstar Rutger Hauer. At the time there was no chance of my achieving any of them. I was broke, and in fact I'd taken out the first overdraft of my life to attend the seminar. I was living in Aberdeen with no job prospects. I had come to the end of my savings and could no longer afford the upkeep of my house nor find a buyer for it. And Rutger Hauer – well, really!

But I did what I was told and suspended my disbelief.

Two weeks after I got back I had a call from a friend who is a television producer saying she was setting up a series called *One Life to Live*. They were doing a feature on cosmetic surgery and wanted someone to have a face-lift on air. Would I be interested? The day after I said 'yes' I had a flyer through the post advertising a series of workshops (exclusively for Equity members and costing only £5.00 each) to be held during the Edinburgh Festival. One of the workshops was being led by, yes, Rutger Hauer. The week after that my brother called from New Zealand to say that he and his wife were sending two airline tickets as a Christmas present for my son and myself to spend two months with them over the holiday period. They'd arranged the flights so that we went via Los Angeles and came back via Hong Kong (round the world). Six weeks later I sold the house to two very nice people for a very nice profit.

Six months after that goal-setting exercise I was sitting on a plane on my way to New Zealand. My furniture was in store ready for my move back to London on my return. I had not only paid off my debts but I had some savings in the building society. I had a brand new jawline and I'd spent a whole day with Rutger Hauer.

So, don't ask me if I think goal-setting works. I know it does!

Survival Strategy 9
Eating for Energy

The maxim 'You are what you eat' is as true today as ever it was. If you live on doughnuts and chips, you'll be fat, spotty and prone to colds. You'll also be setting yourself up for heart problems, hypertension and an early grave. Fish, fruits and fresh vegetables will keep you slim, sexy and filled with the maximum amount of energy – which is what you need when you're coping with the stress of trying to pull your life back together again.

Ironic, then, that a shock to the system such as being left in the lurch by the one we love often drives us to one of two extremes. Either we lose our appetite altogether or we turn to food for comfort and end up resembling a sumo wrestler's fatter sister.

If your weight is stable but you feel sluggish and half-dead all the time, you may also need to rethink your eating patterns.

Here is a simple guide to healthy eating:

1. Focus on *diet*, not *dieting*. Dieting is not only a miserable, negative way of getting into shape, it's also self-defeating.

The body, despite what we do to it, remains an amazingly complex piece of apparatus. It is built for self-preservation. Should we swallow something that doesn't agree with us, the body will expel it. When we deprive the body of food, it adjusts to that, too. In the past it was much more common for the average person to go through bouts of starvation: long winter months when there was no meat or vegetables; times of siege or famine. The miraculous human frame coped with all that by dropping its metabolic level (the rate at which it burns up food for fuel) and making do with less. Even though the industrialized nations now enjoy a greater affluence, the body reacts to deprivation in the same way. When we starve it of the nutrients it needs to function properly (by going on a diet), it shifts down a gear and continues to function on less food.

But here's the catch: when we reach our desired weight (or before, if we have zero willpower) and start to eat normally again, our metabolism takes a while to readjust. The result is that eating what we could before, now makes us gain weight. Our engine is still in low gear. By the time it changes up, the damage has been done. We are fatter than we were before we started. And all because we went on a diet.

Focus instead on healthy eating. And make positive choices: say, 'I'll have a nice crunchy apple,' rather than 'I mustn't eat chocolate cake.'

2. Water content. The body is 80 per cent water and if you suffer from water retention around period time, it can certainly feel like it. But habitual water retention may be the body's way of defending us against our diet. If we clog the tissues with toxins, the body overcompensates in an attempt to wash them away. The way to counteract this is by eating water-rich foods. Fruit, vegetables and freshly squeezed juices will flush out the system naturally. Too much salt also leads to water retention, so take the salt-cellar off the table and cut down the amount you use in cooking. Avoid diuretics unless you want to look like a prune. If you're taking them for pre-menstrual tension, replace potassium lost in the urine by eating a banana a day.

3. Raw foods. Much of the goodness in food is literally

cooked out, so eat as much as you can raw. Raw carrots taste much better than cooked ones anyway, and coleslaw is infinitely tastier than boiled cabbage. Steam vegetables so that the vitamins don't leach out in the cooking water. Bake potatoes or boil them in their skins. Eat a large salad with every meal and avoid barbecues. Those black crusty bits on the spare-ribs that taste so scrumptious can form free radicals which have been linked with cancer.

4. Shopping. Your diet starts in the supermarket, so shop carefully, preferably after a meal. That way you won't be tempted to fill your trolley with cream cakes and convenience food.

If you're home alone, and about 11.00 p.m. you have an overwhelming urge to eat the piece of strawberry cheesecake in the fridge, don't think you're abnormal. The trick is not to have it in the fridge in the first place.

5. Coffee. If you snap at the children, are rude to shop assistants and generally feel as though your hair is standing on end by bedtime, it may have nothing to do with your present situation. You may just be drinking too much coffee. Caffeine is a stimulant and an overdose can give you the shakes and induce that terrible feeling of nervous anxiety which settles in the middle of the solar plexus and won't go away. If you're a real addict, start by cutting out the last cup of the day and work backwards until the only one you're drinking is the mug that gets you out of bed in the morning. As your diet improves you'll find you become less dependent and may be able to cut this one out too. Never drink coffee after 8.00 p.m. if you want a decent night's sleep.

Don't replace your coffee with endless cups of tea. Tea has caffeine in it, too. Try skim milk, juices, herb teas or just plain water.

6. Digestive enzymes. Another reason for dicky tummy may be that you are secreting too much acid in an attempt to digest a diet of over-processed, undernourishing junk. Altering the diet has to be the first priority, but you can lend a hand with a course of digestive enzyme tablets which you can get from your health food shop. Don't take proprietary dyspepsia tablets. Their effect is to neutralize the acid in the stomach but the stomach's reaction is to produce *more* acid to try to neutralize the pill.

Use your common sense: if you have persistent heartburn or discomfort after eating, check with your doctor that you don't have gall-bladder trouble or an incipient ulcer.

7. Food-combining. This works on the premise that the stomach needs to secrete different enzymes to digest protein and carbohydrates, and so you shouldn't eat protein and carbohydrates at the same sitting. Some foods, like vegetables, are neutral and can be combined with either protein or carbohydrates. Fruit should always be eaten alone, preferably between meals. So you can eat a baked potato (carbohydrate) with vegetables or a large salad (neutral) or a steak (protein) with the same, but you shouldn't eat steak (protein) and chips (carbohydrate) together. Beans (neutral) on toast (carbohydrate) are fine. Raquel Welch swears by food-combining as does Sir John Mills. This is a very rough guide, but if you'd like to know more there are several excellent books on the subject (see Further Reading).

8. Wonder foods. Honey, ginseng, blackstrap molasses, yeast – at some time each of these has been hailed as a miracle food. So far no authenticated studies have shown there is any truth in the extravagant claims made for any of them. Omega 5 in fish oil is said to be wonderful for the arteries, which is why Eskimos, who eat a 90 per cent fatty diet, have such a low incidence of heart disease. It also helps lubricate arthritic joints. During the war everyone was issued with cod-liver oil and orange juice to keep winter colds at bay. As with all these things moderation is the key. Don't emulate the man who, having been told that carrots were good for him, proceeded to drink ten pints of carrot juice a day, eventually turned bright yellow and died of Vitamin A poisoning.

9. A little of what you fancy. Try not to feel sorry for yourself. Don't say, 'This new eating regime means I'm never going to be able to eat another mouthful of peanut-brittle ice-cream.' Never is a long time. Provided you stick to the rules most of the time, you can allow yourself the occasional slip (or chip) on special occasions. Just be extra careful the next day.

10. Junk food. Sweeties play havoc with the blood-sugar level. Burgers are like lard in a bun. Both are empty calories, as is alcohol, and the artificial high they induce will be followed by an equally miserable low. The instant fix isn't worth it and violent fluctuations of your blood-sugar levels can knock the system out of sync and leave you with diabetes in later life.

11. Diet aids. Sugar-free gum, appetite suppressants, cigarettes – none of them can replace that good old-fashioned commodity: willpower. The cheapest diet aid around is a large glass of water. Taken before a meal, it will fill your stomach up so you don't want to eat so much. The most effective diet aid is to say, 'No, thank you,' to second helpings, chocolate-chip cookies, that extra gin and tonic. Try it. It gets easier with practice.

12. Common sense. If you are five foot one and have a pelvis that guarantees an easy time in the labour ward, resign yourself to the fact that you will never, no matter how you manipulate your diet, end up looking like Elle Macpherson. Keep a sense of proportion – yours. What to aim for is the best possible version of you that there is.

13. Exercise. Working out won't necessarily make you lose weight. Aerobic exercise will raise your metabolic rate so that you burn up calories faster. Strength work will build up lean muscle, which uses more calories at rest than flab. A combination of sensible eating and moderate *regular* exercise is the key to maximizing your body image. Over time lean muscle will replace fat, making you more streamlined. If you don't lose much weight, don't despair. Muscle weighs more than fat, so you'll look slimmer even if you don't weigh any less.

14. Eating habits. Often it's not what people eat but how they eat that does the damage. Do you head for the fridge every time you hit a problem? Do you pick when you're preparing food? Do you devour the kids' leftovers instead of putting them in the bin? Do certain things like sitting down in front of the TV trigger your tastebuds? Be aware of what you're doing. Change your habits and, without doing anything else, you could cut 500 unwanted calories a day from your diet. That is equivalent to virtually a stone in three months.

If you're underweight and can't face a full meal, nibbling is a good way to put on pounds. Just make sure your nibbles are the healthy kind, crudités and plain yoghurt, cheese on toast, dried fruit and nuts, rather than crisps, biscuits and sweets.

15. Carbohydrates. It used to be thought that all you needed to do to lose weight was cut out bread and potatoes. Wrong. The right kind – known as complex carbohydrates (wholemeal bread, pasta, brown rice, pulses, root vegetables and bananas) – will give you energy, fill you up and, because the energy is released slowly, stop you snacking between meals. The wrong sort (sugar, white bread, sausages, sweets, cake, jam, biscuits and most junk food) will make you gain weight and contains about as much nutritional value as sawdust.

16. Fibre. Keeps everything on the move. Stops your bowels from silting up, which, should it happen, allows toxins that should be eliminated to leach back into the system through the colon walls. Think roughage: cereals, raw veg, salads, fruit and baked potatoes.

17. Protein. A must for healthy bones and tissues, yet we need much less than was formerly supposed. Two small helpings a day of meat, fish, eggs, cheese and/or milk is ample for an adult who has stopped growing.

18. Vitamins and minerals. It is now recognized that a good, balanced diet will provide all the vitamins and minerals the body needs. However, if you are rundown and under par, a two-month course of a combined vitamin/mineral pill once a day is a positive option.

19. Fat. Fat makes fat – need I say more? The Western diet is heavily overloaded with it. Redress the balance by changing to skimmed milk, water-based spreads and low-fat cheese and yoghurt. Cut down on fatty meats, like pork, in favour of chicken and fish (not the smoked variety), and go carefully with nuts and avocados. Avoid mayonnaise, peanut butter and biscuits. And never eat cream.

20. Sleep. If you don't get enough, you may be overeating to 'keep yourself going'. Don't misread the signals: the body is saying 'rest' not 'food'. Try to get an average of eight hours if you can. If your sleep pattern is erratic, allow yourself a nap in the afternoon. Much better for you than a cup of tea and a chocolate digestive.

If you're over- or underweight to begin with, you'll find that, as a side effect of adopting more healthy eating patterns, your weight will stabilize too. And your energy should increase 100 per cent.

19 • Self-Support

Work can be one of the most rewarding areas of life. And not just financially, for rewards come in many guises. Job satisfaction, increased self-worth, the knowledge that your efforts are making the world a better place, not just for yourself, but for everyone around you. The ideal is to work at something you love, something you are good at, something which, if you didn't need the money, you'd be happy to do for free. This may not be an option now, but it's something to aim for.

So, looking ahead to a better future and, assuming that you have to work and that you do need the money, what is the best way to go about getting a job and enjoying it?

First look to your skills and interests. What are you good at? What do you enjoy?

Happily, you need no longer be a surrogate male to be a success in business. Nor do you need to wait for someone to give you a job before you can start earning. If you are untrained or over a certain age, you may be told by certain employers or career advisors that you are unemployable. Take no notice. The people who make such statements are not only narrow-minded and blinkered, they are behind the times. There is no longer such a thing as a job for life. Congratulate yourself that, in a world where more and more people are having to face unlooked-for early retirement or unexpected redundancy, you are ahead of the game.

If no one will give you a job, you can create a job of your own. You have choices. Find out what they are by doing a breakdown of your assets. You'll be amazed at what you've got going for you.

First list the practical things at your disposal. What do you own that might be put to good use in your search for financial independence? Do you have a house, a phone, a sewing machine, a knitting machine, a washing machine? A word-processor, a kitchen, a car?

Now list your mental attributes. Do you have any qualifications? What are your aptitudes? Are you a leader or a follower, an organizer, a nurturer or a communicator? What skills do you possess? Can you teach, write, cook, keep house? Do you like children, dogs, gardening, embroidery, origami? No matter how trivial or seemingly irrelevant, get it on paper.

Once you've got your lists you'll have some idea of what you want to do on a permanent basis.

Having done that you can look at one of four options:

1. A job.
2. A career.
3. A profession.
4. A business.

A Job

Suppose you have no training, no assets and no money. Obviously the niceties of career development will need to be set aside temporarily. You will need to get a job as quickly as possible. Look at your lists and aim for one that's relevant. Don't let the current unemployment figures deter you. Whatever your age, experience or level of education, if you are willing to work, there *are* jobs out there.

Where?

- At the job centre. Go down straight away and sign on.

- In the paper. Check out the situations vacant columns of both the local and national papers (at the library).

- At the newsagent's. Scan the wanted ads in the window. There may be only baby-sitting or cleaning on offer, but it's a start.

- Word of mouth. Ask – at your children's school, for example. If they do dinners on site, they might want help in the kitchen. Let all your local shops and businesses know you're available. If they have a vacancy behind the counter or answering the phone, they'd much rather fill it without the expense of advertising the post. My son did this at the local cinema. He asked whether there was any fill-in work before he started college in September. The manager asked him to put his application in writing and he was taken on. His numeracy and people skills improved immensely, he saved enough to cover his college expenses and, when he did start his course, he was able to stay on three evenings a week to supplement his income.

  Consider every opening as an opportunity that may lead to greater things. I have a friend who went to an oil firm as a tea-lady and ended up travelling the world as nanny to the managing director's children.

What kind of job?

Out of the house. Look for jobs with built-in extras:

- Bar work – free meals and social intercourse.
- Usherette – free movies or plays.
- Waitress – free meals and tips.

Self Support

- Shop assistant – most large chains give discount on in-store products and, if you like the retail trade and show aptitude and enthusiasm, even the humblest beginnings can lead on to greater things, such as becoming a buyer.

- Leaflet distribution – flexible hours and you can use down time to learn by listening to educational tapes.

- Nude model at your local art school – pleasant environment and leaves the brain free to plan for the future.

- Cleaning – early-morning work leaves the day free to write bestseller, re-train or start your own business.

- Taxi-driver, if you have your own car and a clean licence – flexible hours. Drop the kids at school and get on with it. Work days and you'll avoid drunks.

- Other options: shelf stacking, supermarket check-out, ladies' room attendant in posh hotel, tea-lady, dinner-lady, lollipop lady.

In the house. Don't do piece-work (envelope stuffing and the like). It's *very* badly paid. Instead aim to offer a service. Depending on what's on your 'assets' list you could:

- Let rooms.
- Do telephone sales or data collecting.
- Dress- or curtain-making.
- Repairs to same.
- Article writing.
- CV writing.
- Manuscript or thesis typing.
- Baking (for local tea-rooms).
- Washing and ironing (for students or local bed-sit tenants).

Advertise in local shop windows or in the free small ads in the press, and by word of mouth. Remember that any of the above could be developed into a home-based business (see Chapter 20).

At job level you will only be looking at subsistence wages. Think ahead from survival to abundance. Try to move onwards and upwards as soon as possible. Don't be depressed by lowly beginnings. If you've never worked before, a low-paid job with little responsibility can ease you into the workforce without initially fazing you. But look on such a job as a stepping stone to better things, rather than a cul-de-sac.

A Career

If you've never had a career, you can train for one. You may have had one which you loved and were good at, but if you've had a long break, you may need to retrain.

Depending on your level of expertise and the amount of money you have available, training can be short-term or long-term. Opt for the best and fastest. Courses which you have to pay for yourself will generally be shorter. There are some excellent private word-processing courses which, if you've had previous typing skills, could have you out temping within the month. If you choose to cover the same ground at a college of further education, it could take you a year. Remember that time is money, so the sooner you can get yourself out into the marketplace, the better.

For longer training, like a college course in beauty therapy or hairdressing (or word-processing), there are often grants available for mature students or women returning to work. Check with your library or local education authority.

Consider out of the ordinary training options which

maximize your intuitive and nurturing skills. Counsellor. Hypnotherapist. Alternative practitioner (aromatherapist, reflexologist, masseuse). Exercise instructor. Florist. The easiest way to find out about such courses is to buy an appropriate magazine and look in the ads at the back. Send for the brochures of at least half a dozen courses. Check them out for price, availability (when the next one starts), pre-requirements (you may need a certain level of education before you're taken on) and location (nearest your home). Check also which of them is affiliated to the appropriate national accreditation body. You don't want to spend your hard-earned time and money on a diploma that isn't worth the paper it's written on.

Certain jobs may carry the benefit of on-going training at the company's expense. Hairdressing, the retail trade, and any of the leisure or service industries often allow you to acquire extra qualifications while you are earning a wage. The usual options are either to spend one day a week at college or have regular fortnightly stints away at training centres.

Night school is always an option, albeit a challenging one, if you are holding down a dead-end job which doesn't offer the above facility. Gaining extra qualifications this way can be hard but many people have used evening classes as their first rung up the ladder to eventual success.

If you have a skill like playing the guitar or speaking a language, you can supplement a meagre grant while you are studying by giving classes from home in the evenings. Remember that group work is more lucrative than individual lessons. If your normal fee is £7.00 an hour, think about taking half a dozen pupils at once at a fiver each. As long as everyone in the class gets their money's worth, there's nothing reprehensible about you making £30.00 an hour rather than £7.00.

A Profession

Again, if you had one before, you may want to take it up again. Almost certainly, though, you will need to do some kind of refresher course. The Open University is a way to do this if you have to work while you study.

If you want to take up a profession you may have to take a degree course. Remember you are looking at three to four years of your life, but don't be put off by killjoys who say you're too old. I have a cousin who, at fifty-nine and newly retired from the BBC, is taking a degree in criminal law. The experience has opened up her whole life and given her an entirely new set of friends. And ignore anyone who says studying is harder when you're older. The brain only stops functioning when you do.

If you married young and don't have any A levels, you may have to do an extra foundation course before you apply for university. It all depends on how determined you are. Being short on education has nothing to do with being short on brains. Apply to your local university for entrance criteria and take it from there. It may be ten years before you're a doctor. But if you don't take the plunge, where will you be in ten years?

Placements. If you are an older graduate who is having difficulty getting a placement try ARP – the Association of Retired Persons Over 50. They have access to certain recruitment agencies which specialize in older professionals. And enquire of such age-related magazines as *Choice*, *Active Life*, *050*. They are a fund of knowledge and may be able to supply you with back numbers which have informative articles.

A Business

You never make *real* money working for someone else. For information on how to start your own business, see Chapter 20.

Portfolio People

It used to be thought that if you were a jack of all trades you would, of necessity, be master of none. Thankfully, this is no longer true. If you have various skills and possess a low boredom threshold, you might want to become a 'portfolio person'. Portfolio people are those who can turn their hands to several things so that, should there be a slump in the demand for one of their skills, they have several others to fall back on.

For example, when I had my exercise studio, December was always a down time. In December people are in party-mode; they want to pig out and have fun. As far as the average exerciser is concerned, their abdominals can go hang until the day of reckoning – January 1st. If I'd been depending on work-out clientele to see me through Christmas, we'd have been feasting on a head of lettuce and a box of small eggs instead of the traditional turkey. Luckily, December is one of the busiest months in the voice-over industry – everyone wants to advertise their festive products and hedge their bets by informing folk of the January sales to come. Since radio and TV voice-over work is another part of my 'portfolio', I was able to cash in on that while my studio income was at a low.

As long as you don't diversify too much and are reasonably organized, having several strings to your bow can only be to your advantage. I know a man who is an architect, a counsellor, a masseur, a consultant to industry and an author, all on different days of the week. He subsidizes his less lucrative (but perhaps more enjoyable) skills with income from his high-earning days. And he's one of the nicest, most together people I know.

All Hands to the Plough

Having their own income gives children a sense of self-worth and a modicum of independence. Encourage them to get a Saturday job (they'd only be watching the box otherwise). Getting a regular pay-packet gives them some control over their life and saves you forking out pocket money when times are hard. It also teaches them the value of money. If they have to save up for a new video game, you can be sure they'll appreciate it more than if someone else bought it.

If they're over sixteen, they can buy their own trainers (quite a consideration when the cost of a pair of Reeboks could feed a family of four for a fortnight), CDs and trips to McDonald's with their mates. If they're under sixteen they can at least buy their own comics and sweets.

They don't have to be paper boys or girls. Bad pay, bad hours and early rising in all weathers is hardly going to instil a love of work in them. Try to encourage them to be entrepreneurial – cleaning cars, mowing lawns or running errands. Like you, they'll stick at something they enjoy and don't feel exploited by doing.

Incidentally, if they *do* get a job, don't take any money from them. Most children work hard at school. If they are going to do extra in their own time, they deserve to get the benefit from it. The days of child-slavery are dead and you are not Fagin.

20 • Business Sense

Except for a six-month stint after I left drama school, working in an Oxford Street department store (on handbags and small leathers), I have never had what my dad would term 'a proper job'. I traded in the security of a weekly pay packet and promissory pension for the dubious joys of self-employment and doing something I loved. In the last thirty years I have come through more financial troughs than I would care to mention. I have slept in the Ritz and dossed in the back of a car (only once, but once is certainly enough!). I have travelled the world as a singer, fronted TV quiz shows and opened supermarkets, had eight books published, sold a screenplay and a TV series and run a successful exercise business. I have also failed auditions, coped with rejection slips and taught half-empty classes on snowy days when not even an Eskimo would have ventured forth. But I have never been bored. Nor have I ever regretted my decision.

In business I've found that there are five stages to ultimate success. You don't have to follow all of them right through; you can stop at whichever point is comfortable. That's the beauty of it. How successful you are depends not on fate or chance or the market; it depends on you.

Here are the five stages:

1. Become self-employed. Offer goods or services.

2. Specialize or diversify.

3. Train and/or employ others.

4. Develop new outlets, skills or areas.

5. Develop product.

As an example, let's take my own exercise business which grew out of a hobby that I loved. My initial aspirations were no higher than to keep myself in shape without having to shell out for classes. If people would pay me rather than the other way round, I thought I would be quite happy. But then, like Topsy, the whole thing 'just growed'.

1. *After my teacher training I didn't take a job with a fitness club – I took a chance. I hired premises, advertised, and ran my own classes. Even after I'd paid my overheads the profits were three times higher than my salary would have been. I started teaching three classes a week, then built it up to eight. I soon realized that when you are working for yourself, income is finite – if you make £200 working an eight-hour day, you will have to work a 16-hour day to make £400. What I needed at this point was a strategy. A way not to work harder, but to be smarter.*

2. *I decided to specialize. Instead of offering the same classes as everyone else, I picked a section of the market which wasn't being covered – seniors. I retrained, and became the recognized authority in the area. This maximized my client base. I developed courses, fronted workshops and seminars. These commanded higher fees than classes, so I was able to generate more income for the same outlay of time.*

3. *The next stage was to train and employ other teachers to take more classes. Profit escalated.*

4. *I started to write articles for magazines specializing in fitness; I became fitness consultant on over-sixties' exercise to the local health board; was invited to appear on TV and speak on radio*

> *programmes; wrote and recorded my own series for cable television. I took certification as a personal trainer and moved into the business sector, where I could command higher fees. I instigated classes further afield; consulted and lectured nationwide.*
>
> 5. *Finally I began to 'produce product'. The articles became books. I made a relaxation tape. If I'd stayed in the business longer, I might well have made a video. I may do yet. I was now making money while I slept.*

Then my old man left me and I allowed myself and the whole enterprise to fall apart. But we live and learn!

Note that the five stages to ultimate success necessitate constant re-education and the learning of new skills. You get nothing for nothing. If you rest on your laurels, you will run out of steam and others will overtake you. If you invest time, energy and enthusiasm, if you *love* your subject and care for your customers, you will be repaid one hundred fold, not only in money but in job satisfaction.

Most small businesses are selling either goods or services. As an example of a goods-based concern let's apply the blueprint to a home-based cookery business:

> 1. *Start in your kitchen (no outlay) making cakes for the local tea-rooms.*
>
> 2. *Specialize in something which you do wonderfully, say, lemon meringue pies. Sell only lemon meringue pies to all the local tea-rooms. This simplifies your shopping list and allows you to make large batches of just one thing. Teach your daughter, sister or mother to make the pies to increase turnover and cover for you in case you're sick.*
>
> 3. *Employ a washer-upper to take the dirty work off your hands and a weekly cleaner so that you don't have to worry about the housework. Maybe a driver to deliver pies? Invest the time saved by taking a short business management course (many*

> local TECs or small business enterprise groups offer this kind of part-time further education free). Invest the money saved in company image – a recognizable logo and headed stationery.
>
> 4. Approach the local supermarket about selling your pies. If they sell well, approach the regional marketing director about selling throughout the chain. At this point, and provided you get the contract, think about finding premises and taking on a professional pastry-cook and some staff to deal with increased turnover.
>
> 5. Open classy tea-rooms at front of new premises selling all the other wonderful cakes you can bake. Sell extra lines to supermarket. Open another two premises in adjacent towns. Franchise tea-rooms nationwide. Set up a distribution system. Float shares on stock-market. Sell business for several million pounds. Retire to the Bahamas.

Practicalities

You don't have to become a limited company to start your own business – although this is an option. You can work as a sole trader until you start taking on employees. Even then, if you hire people who are themselves self-employed, and get them to sign a statement saying they are liable for their own tax and national insurance, you can retain your independence. Many leisure clubs do this by hiring out studios to teachers who are responsible for their own income.

For a small fee you can register your trading name. But even that's not necessary unless you think someone unscrupulous might pinch your business or bring that name into disrepute.

It's not expensive to form a limited company but there is a certain amount of hassle involved in that you will have to send audited books to Companies' House every year. The advantage of a limited company is that should you go bust, you have limited liability, i.e. the company is responsible for debts, not you personally. If you go bust as a sole trader, your assets would be forfeit and you might have to go bankrupt. One of the perks of having your own company is that you can write company director on your passport. One of the disadvantages is the amount of junk mail you'll receive from people trying to sell you anything from saunas to photocopiers to financial services to overpriced workshops.

Liabilities

As a self-employed person you will have to pay tax twice yearly (in January and July) and national insurance (currently the self-employed stamp works out at around £75.00 a quarter) once every three months. Depending on how much you make, extra national insurance will be added to your tax bill.

In theory you can fill in your tax returns yourself. In practice, it's worth every penny to get yourself a good accountant to do it for you. It used to be the case that you put your books in at the end of the year and paid tax the following year. As of December 1996 though, you will have to do a Mystic Meg and estimate what you *think* you're going to make and pay the tax in advance! As if this wasn't bad enough, those of us already in the system will have to pay two years' tax at once. In theory, if you overpay you will get a rebate. In practice, the government will have the use of your money, interest free, for twelve months. How do they get away with it? Anyway, take my advice and get an accountant. And make sure you set aside 25 per cent for tax as you go along. Put it in a separate deposit account so you get some interest on it. That way you won't spend it and get lumbered with an enormous bill that you can't pay.

You can forget about VAT until your turnover (not your profits – make sure you're clear on that) is in excess of £35,000 a year. Again, you need to estimate up front whether you think you're going to make more than that in the following quarter and register straight away. Your accountant will put you right. The penalties for late payment of VAT are Draconian. So if you're happy with a certain level of business, you might want to make the VAT threshold your expansion cut-off point.

Funding

Some people don't go into business because they think they'll have to do cash-flow projections and take out bank loans and pay exorbitant interest rates and have nervous breakdowns. Some people have the nervous breakdown when their bank manager turns down their request, despite all the time and expense they've gone to getting the aforementioned cash-flow forecast drawn up by an 'expert'.

The trick is not to borrow at all unless you have to. If you need an essential piece of equipment (like a knitting machine) to get started, buy it on hire purchase so it pays for itself as you use it, or ask family or friends to stake you.

Otherwise, it's much better to allow the business to grow in its own time, funding itself as it goes along. Somewhere in the future you might want to take that quantum leap where extra funding would catapult you into the big time, but right at the beginning it's rarely necessary. Also, it's much easier to raise a loan on a proven enterprise looking to expand than it is on an untried idea. Bank managers are very conservative – especially when dealing with single women.

What you *don't* spend, when launching yourself as the new Betty Crocker or Kaffe Fasset or Jane Fonda, is more important than what you do. You are testing the water, to see whether your service or product is in demand. So to start with you should keep your overheads low. Ask yourself, would you be inspired to work a fourteen-hour day just to pay off an overdraft?

So – don't sign leases for expensive premises if you can work from home. Don't lash out on the latest word-processor if there's still life in the old one. Don't take on assistants until you get to the point where you are really stretched. And don't forget that when you *do* have to buy or replace equipment it's tax deductible. Hooray!

Initial Investment

I had £2,000 in savings when I started my exercise business. I chose to 'speculate to accumulate' and blew it all on the following items. I offer them for your consideration:

- Training – the best I could get.

- Self-promotion. No matter how excellent your goods or service is, if no one knows you're there, they won't buy it. Advertising is very expensive but if your business is something with a human interest angle you may be able to persuade a local journalist to interview you: 'Local girl launches lemon meringues with great-grandmama's recipe found in attic – "Every time I bake one I feel she's looking over my shoulder," said Miss X. 'People don't read ads unless they are specifically looking for something. But they read and believe copy. If you don't have a friend in the press, write a few paragraphs yourself and send it in to the news desk. Editors are always trying to fill space. If you have a photo (of you or great-grandmama) so much the better.

    Of all the methods I tried (newspapers, leaflet drops,

posters), local radio brought the greatest response. TV ads are financially out of the question, and most people get up to make a cup of tea when the commercials come on anyway, but with radio you have not only kudos but a captive audience as well. People tune in while doing the housework, in their cars, at the beach, on a picnic. It's a very effective way of getting your message across.

When putting ads in shop windows, try to be artistic and inventive. A little colour works wonders. If you have kids, get them to do it for you. They can cut out words from magazines and make up a notice like criminals do with ransom notes. Great fun. Make fifty photocopies down the library and stick them up on every available space. Or send the kids out to post them in every letter-box for a radius of two miles.

- A logo – a phrase or design which is individual to you.
- Business stationery – letterheads, envelopes, calling cards.
- Equipment – leotards, music, sound system.
- Licences and liability insurance (*very* important whatever you do).
- Membership of professional bodies – for credibility and networking and access to continuing education, conferences, etc.

As a matter of interest, I made my investment back within three months of opening.

You only need premises when you've established a market. That's the time to splash out on a hairdressing or petcare salon, a retail outlet, exercise studio or tea-room. At the beginning try to get the shortest lease possible. If you make a tremendous success of it, the rent will go up accordingly, I'm afraid, but if something outside your control conspires to scupper the enterprise, then you can get out with the maximum speed and the minimum expense.

Another good idea is to hire rooms by the hour (if you are offering a service) in an already established practice. That way you won't be paying rates or utilities or have any outgoings at holiday times. You will also have the advantage of shared advertising and one phone or receptionist for all.

Sample Business Ideas

Go back to your list of assets. The following list of possibilities should get your mind working:

- **House.** Lodgers or bed and breakfast. Classes (English, guitar). Therapy room (to let or for your own use after qualifying as an alternative practitioner).

- **Sewing Machine.** Dressmaking. (Specialize in one thing: I have a fantastic blouson jacket which I bought at a craft fair.) Patchwork quilts, cushion covers, throws. Curtains. Repairs.

- **Knitting machine.** Jumpers, jackets, rainbow-coloured scarves. Wallhangings, tapestries. Specialization idea: children's jumpers with names on. Expansion idea: outworkers on piece-work. Great for older people with skills who like to knit and could do with the extra money!

- **Washing machine.** Laundry for students or local bed-sit tenants. Move up to contract for guest-houses and hotels. Specialization idea: leaflet businesses with a high percentage of bachelor males, offering to launder and deliver shirts. Employ someone to iron. Expansion ideas: buy a chain of launderettes (quantity) or a dry cleaner's specializing in couture garments (quality).

- **Word-processor.** If you're creative, articles, short stories, books (factual – passing on skills/experiences; fiction – romance, sf, thrillers). If you're practical, typing services (manuscripts and theses) or outworking for large firms. Expansion idea: desk-top publishing.

- **Kitchen.** Cater parties. Make and deliver sandwiches for local businesses. Give cookery classes (for men who can't boil an egg, newly weds ditto). Make candles to sell at craft fairs. Shampoo pets.

- **Car.** Chauffeuring (meeting businessmen from airport). Taking services out to the customer – gardening, cleaning, hairdressing or petcare.

- **Garden.** If you have green fingers cultivate homegrown vegetables or flowers or herbs for sale to shops or at local markets or from your garage on Saturday mornings. If you don't have green fingers but like animals, think about a run of free-range chickens for fresh eggs or some kennels for boarding out pets.

So there you are. You don't have to be an international tycoon to start your own business. If you have a good idea, are prepared to put in the time, care about your clients and give true value for money, there's absolutely no reason why you shouldn't be a success. The challenge is in knowing that nobody is going to bail you out. Being in business is the ultimate responsibility. So pick something you love. Then the long, hard hours won't seem so long. Just wonderfully worthwhile.

Survival Strategy 10
Futures Checklist

What happens if you get sick, grow old, have an accident? Hope for the best – but prepare for the worst.

Below is a checklist of things you should get organized as soon as you're settled and have money coming in:

Insurance
- Life.
- Health.
- House. (Buildings and contents if you own your property; contents if you rent.)
- Car.

Savings

Pay off 10 per cent of your debts, HP, overdraft. Put away 10 per cent of the savings you make on the interest payments. If you have a job rather than a business, have the 10 per cent deducted at source. Otherwise put 5 per cent in a deposit or short-term account for unexpected outgoings (your sister gets married and you need to buy a toaster) and 5 per cent in a long-term investment (such as National Savings) where you can't reach it. The longer the investment, the higher the interest rate tends to be. Interest rates are also stepped depending on how much money is in the account (the rich get more and the poor get less).

Places to put your savings:

- Building societies or banks.
- National Savings or government bonds.
- Tessas or PEPS.
- Pensions.
- Shares or Unit trusts.
- Property.

If you know nothing about money, educate yourself by scanning the money pages of your newspaper. Or get a financial advisor. Make sure you're getting the best rate of interest. It can vary enormously. Do your homework. If you decide to plump for a building society, check your *Yellow Pages*, give at least half a dozen a call and ask them to send brochures. That way you can compare and contrast in the comfort of your own home, away from any sales pressure or hype.

Spread your investments rather than putting all your precious eggs in one basket (think of BCCI!).

Make a Will
This is essential if you have children and/or a life insurance policy or property. It is important even if you feel you don't have anything much to leave. Your net worth is probably more than you realize and if you don't sort out who gets what now, no matter how little there is, it will go to lawyers.

You can get 'do it yourself' will forms from any stationer but it's worth the small investment and the peace of mind to have it done by a professional. Contact the Citizens Advice Bureau for where to find a suitable solicitor.

Tax and National Insurance
If you are self-employed, don't forget to squirrel it away (in your short-term account) against the day of payment.

Benefits
If you are entitled to any, don't be proud – claim them! Don't dip into your nest-egg unless you have to. If you are self-employed, you won't be able to collect dole but you can get sick pay if you're struck down by the lurgy. And the cost of your stamp will be paid, contributing to your pension.

Pensions
As we go to press, Parliament is about to change the law on pensions. Currently a man can abandon a woman he has lived with all their adult lives and take any private pension with him. She has no entitlement. If she has opted out of the state scheme as well, she won't even qualify for old age pension. This iniquitous piece of legislation is soon to be reversed. If you are affected by it, you might want to consider putting a hold on any divorce proceedings until after the bill is passed, as unfortunately it will not apply retrospectively.

If humanly possible, invest in a pension of your own. Depending on your age, this should be anything from 10 per cent to 30 per cent of your income (the older you are the more you need to invest to collect a decent stipend when you retire). Consult an independent financial advisor rather than someone tied to one company's product. That way you're more likely to get the best deal for you (rather than them).

Mad Money
Set aside 10 per cent of whatever you earn to spend on sheer enjoyment. Otherwise, why bother? Even something as small as a Saturday night pizza with double anchovies and a video to go will send a message to your subconscious that there's enough coming in for you to splurge on the occasional treat. Otherwise you run the risk of feeling constantly on the edge of penury even after your financial situation has improved.

Try to think of your 'futures' as an Aladdin's cave of riches rather than an emergency fund. If you don't, not only will you not enjoy your hard-earned wealth, you'll keep inventing emergencies to gobble it up. Money is just another form of energy. Having a bit spare should make you feel better – not worse. Enjoy it, and you own it. Worry about it, and it owns you.

Epilogue

Wherever you are in life, you can start today to make that life better. Don't be a martyr. No matter how abandoned and destitute you feel, you are still a millionaire compared to nine tenths of the world's population. If you feel miserable and put upon and hopeless and helpless, remind yourself that you are not living in a cardboard box. Nor are you at the mercy of some avaricious warlord or bloodthirsty dictator.

Instead of wallowing in self-obsession and moaning about what a raw deal the universe has dealt you, try saying 'thanks' for all the wonderful things you *do* have and for all the unlimited possibilities on offer. The only thing stopping you getting over this thing is yourself.

Live in an attitude of gratitude. Think abundance rather than lack. Focus on your health, strength, intelligence, hope for the future. Look outward rather than in.

Half-way into the first awful (sorry – challenging) year of my abandonment, my daughter Sara had a little boy – Benjamin Indiana Sheppard. My first grandson. And suddenly everything slotted into place. His birth ensured my immortality. Why? Because you're not really dead until everyone who knew you has passed on too. Not even then if you leave behind something which contains your essence: a painting or a book or a cushion cover – think of all those lovely Elizabethan samplers stitched so lovingly by hands long since crumbled to dust. We live on in other people's memories, in stories (apocryphal or otherwise), anecdotes, sayings, photographs, letters and recipes.

My daughter has ensured that, barring accidents and given the expected life-span of citizens of the twenty-first century, I will be around, if only in spirit and in the gene-pool of baby Ben, until the year 2100!

I am immortal. And so are you.

Here are five empowering thoughts to stick on your mirror:

1. The world is a wonderful place.

2. The universe provides.

3. Today is the first day of the rest of my life.

4. I am a lovable human being and I deserve the best.

5. I will survive!

Further Reading

Hidden Power for Human Problems, Frederick Bailes, Prentice Hall Press
You Can Heal Your Life, Louise L. Hay, Eden Grove Editions
Feel the Fear and Do It Anyway, Susan Jeffers, Random House
Creative Visualisation, Shakti Gawain, Bantam New Age Books
Do It – A Guide to Living your Dreams, John-Roger and Peter McWilliams, Thorsons
You Can't Afford the Luxury of a Negative Thought, John-Roger and Peter McWilliams, Thorsons
The Silva Mind Control Method, José Silva
Unlimited Power, Anthony Robbins, Simon and Schuster
Awaken the Giant Within, Anthony Robbins, Simon and Schuster
Think and Grow Rich, Napoleon Hill, Wilshire Book Company
As You Think, James Allen, New World Library
Believe You Can, Allan Carmichael, Concept Books
The Celestine Prophecy, James Redfield, Bantam Books
The Road Less Travelled, M. Scott Peck, Arrow Books
How to Think Like a Millionaire, Charles-Albert Poissant (with Christian Godefroy), Thorsons
Superwoman, Shirley Conran, Penguin
Futurewoman, Shirley Conran and Elizabeth Sidney, Penguin
The Positive Woman, Gael Lindenfield, Thorsons
The Complete Book of Massage, Claire Maxwell Hudson, Dorling Kindersley
The Aromatherapy Handbook, Danielle Ryman, Century Publishing
Earning Money at Home, The Consumers Association
Stress and Relaxation, Jane Madders, Macdonald Optima
The 10-Day Relaxation Plan, Dr Eric Trimmer, Piatkus Books

The Complete Manual of Fitness and Well-Being, ed. Ruth Binney, Macdonald
The Wright Diet, Celia Wright, Grafton Books
Food-Combining for Health, Doris Grant and Jean Joice, Thorsons
Colour Me Beautiful, Carole Jackson, Piatkus Books
Colour Me Beautiful Make-Up Book, Carole Jackson, Piatkus Books
The Complete Style Guide, Mary Spillane, Piatkus Books
Uncoupling: How and Why Relationships Fall Apart, Diane Vaughan, Methuen

Useful Addresses

Chapter 2
Relaxation tapes are available from:
New World Music, Paradise Farm, Westhall, Halesworth,
    Suffolk IP19 8RH. Tel: 0198 678 1682

Chapter 5
National Retreat Centre, Central Hall, 256 Bermondsey Street,
    London SE1 3UJ. Tel: 0171 357 7736

Chapter 7
Worldwide Exchange Club, 13 Knightsbridge Gardens,
    London N13 5PG. Tel: 0171 589 6055
Vacation Services Inc., 960 Los Valecitos Boulevard, Suite 102,
    San Marcos, California 92069, USA. Tel: 001 619 471 2426
Country Cousins, 10a Market Square, West Sussex RH12 1EX.
    Tel: 01403 210 415

Chapter 8
National Debtline, 318 Summer Lane, Newtown, Birmingham
    B19 3RL. Tel: 0121 359 8501

Chapter 12
Great Company, 59 Rupert Street, London W1V 7HN.
    Tel: 0171 278 0328
Solitaire Travel Ltd, 8 Melbourne Street, Royston, Herts
    SG8 7BZ. Tel: 01763 294 344

Chapter 14
Dignity, 16 Brixham Close, Nuneaton, Warwickshire CV11 6YT. Tel: 01203 350 312

Chapter 19
Association of Retired Persons Over 50, Greencoat House, Francis Place, London SW1P 1DZ. Tel: 0171 828 0500

Pecking Order

How Your Place in the Family Affects Your Personality

JOY BERTHOUD

Are you: well-organized and ambitious? laid-back and confident? domineering? anxious to please?

It's not only your genes, social background and education that shape your personality. There is another factor, seldom considered yet highly significant, that influences your interaction with the world: your place in the family. Whether you are an only child, first born, twin, middle child or 'the baby', you are indelibly marked by your position in the pecking order. Every relationship is affected by this fact of life: with parents, siblings, school and work friends, partners – and, eventually, your own children.

Much academic research has been done into this fascinating aspect of family dynamics, and in *Pecking Order* Joy Berthoud sifts the evidence to present an analysis accessible to everyone. To this she has added her own research, including profiles of famous figures from the worlds of politics, sport and the arts. The result is a compelling and eye-opening survey of a subject that touches every one of us.

Gollancz £9.99 pb   0 575 06035 2

The Baby Bible
JULIET LEIGH

The indispensable consumer guide for pregnant women and new mothers.

At last, the answers to the questions that matter to Britain's one million expectant mothers: 'What should I buy?' 'Whom should I listen to?' 'Where can I find specialist advice?'

As soon as you realize you are pregnant, you are faced with a bewildering array of choices: choices in health and childcare, choices in maternity wear and baby products. You're anxious to get it right, but first you have to know:

- What you *really* need
- Which products offer the best value for money
- What to look for when buying second-hand
- How to get the best out of the health service
- Where to turn for help

The Baby Bible tells you everything you need to know about choosing and using all the products and services available to pregnant women and new mothers. It will dispel myths, reassure anxious new parents, and enable you to avoid expensive and dangerous mistakes.

Gollancz £8.99 pb   0 575 06034 4

Married Love
MARIE STOPES

The ground-breaking book that transformed millions of lives in the first half of the century.

First published in 1918, *Married Love* dared to challenge centuries of prejudice, superstition and religious teaching that had made sex, and women's bodies, into a dirty secret. At last, both men and women were freed from their ignorance, encouraged to enjoy sex without shame and to explore women's sexuality.

Married Love went on to sell over a million copies, and was translated into fourteen languages. This major classic – which is of enormous importance in the history of the women's movement, both as the first book of its kind and as a shocking reminder of the repression of women at the turn of the century – has been out of print for over forty years, and has been republished to coincide with a Channel 4 documentary film of Stopes's life.

Gollancz £6.99 pb   0 575 06273 8

My Life
ISADORA DUNCAN

The classic autobiography, still as extraordinary as the woman who wrote it more than sixty years ago.

Isadora Duncan (1877–1927), a remarkable visionary, revolutionized dance in the twentieth century, captivating audiences in Europe, America and Russia with her passionate, innovative, free-flowing style. Frank and open like her dancing, *My Life* describes her notorious love affairs; the tragic deaths of her children; and her total commitment to establishing modern dance as a serious art form, leading the way for other great dance pioneers such as Agnes de Mille and Martha Graham.

Gollancz £8.99   0 575 06250 9

Baby Alarm!
JOHN CRACE

Forget the books that give you practical tips. The ones full of dreary anecdotes about the first time you actually change a nappy or how you get the little beast off to sleep. This is the anxious, secret, hellish world of fatherhood.

It's not about how you behave, but about how you *feel* – and there's an enormous gap between the two. It's about the Freudian terrors that lurk within every nursery; it's about making sure that 'Dada' is your progeny's first utterance whatever the cost; it's about the constant struggle to be Most Important Parent; it's

BABY ALARM!

Fatherhood with attitude.

'John Crace embraces fatherhood with gusto, humour and an admirable ability to say what most new dads cannot'
She magazine

'A truly engaging and, above all, candid account of becoming a dad' *Guardian*

Vista £4.99 pb 0 575 60054 3

Coming shortly in paperback:

Fatherhood
PETER HOWARTH

Of all the thousands of pages published on the subject of pregnancy and childbirth few have been concerned with the experience solely from the father's point of view.

In *Fatherhood*, some of today's finest young writers reflect on this rude process of coming of age – from the very first inklings of male broodiness (it does exist, apparently), through nine months of sitting on the bench spectating, to the nerve-racking primal moment of delivery ... and beyond.

Fatherhood is an eclectic collection of disparate viewpoints – funny, poignant, philosophical and in some cases downright odd – which invites its contributors, and its readers, to wrestle with the fundamental stuff of life. It is essential reading for any man who has found or might find himself listening to those awesome words: 'I think I'm pregnant.'

Contributors include:
Tony Parsons	Stephen Amidon
Robert Newman	Mike Phillips
Douglas Kennedy	John Hegley
Nicholas Lezard	Stephen Bayley

Gollancz £9.99 pb   0 575 06345 9

On Kissing
ADRIANNE BLUE

Original, intelligent, entertaining and sexy. *On Kissing* offers remarkable insight into one of life's greatest pleasures. This book tells why the kiss is one of the most powerful and evocative gestures in Western culture. Adrianne Blue argues convincingly that there is a kiss continuum. A loop of meaning which informs every kiss. Whether of friendship, ritual or love. And in the process she reveals a breathtaking landscape which includes the peaks and valleys of the maternal, the placatory, the spiritual, the metaphorical and the erotic.

The love scenes of Garbo, the yearning of Proust, the sarcasm of Amis, the sensuality of Colette are put into fascinating perspective in a book which maps scientific, artistic and emotional terrain. From anthropology to amour propre, from biology to Byronic greed, from Catullus to cunnilingus, from Freud to Hollywood frontiers, *On Kissing* takes the reader on a compelling voyage of discovery.

Indigo £6.99 pb 0 575 40079 X

VISTA and Gollancz paperbacks are available from all good bookshops or from:

> Cassel C.S.
> Book Service By Post
> PO Box 29, Douglas I-O-M
> IM99 1BQ
> telephone: 01624 670923

While every effort is made to keep prices steady, it is sometimes necessary to increase prices at short notice. Cassell plc reserves the right to show on covers and charge new retail prices which may differ from those advertised in the text or elsewhere.